Raising Curtains
on
Education

Critical Studies in Education and Culture Series

Education and the Welfare State: A Crisis in Capitalism and Democracy
H. Svi Shapiro

Education under Siege: The Conservative, Liberal and Radical Debate over Schooling
Stanley Aronowitz and Henry A. Giroux

Literacy: Reading the Word and the World
Paulo Freire and Donaldo Macedo

The Moral and Spiritual Crisis in Education: A Curriculum for Justice and Compassion
David Purpel

The Politics of Education: Culture, Power and Liberation
Paulo Freire

Popular Culture, Schooling and the Language of Everyday Life
Henry A. Giroux and Roger I. Simon

Teachers As Intellectuals: Toward a Critical Pedagogy of Learning
Henry A. Giroux

Women Teaching for Change: Gender, Class and Power
Kathleen Weiler

Between Capitalism and Democracy: Educational Policy
and the Crisis of the Welfare State
Svi Shapiro

Critical Psychology and Pedagogy: Interpretation of the Personal World
Edmund Sullivan

Pedagogy and the Struggle for Voice: Issues of Language,
Power, and Schooling for Puerto Ricans
Catherine E. Walsh

Learning Work: A Critical Pedagogy of Work Education
Roger I. Simon, Don Dippo, and Arleen Schenke

Cultural Pedagogy: Art/Education/Politics
David Trend

RAISING CURTAINS ON EDUCATION

Drama as a
Site for
Critical Pedagogy

Clar Doyle

CRITICAL STUDIES IN EDUCATION
AND CULTURE SERIES
Edited by Henry A. Giroux and Paulo Freire

BERGIN & GARVEY
WESTPORT, CONNECTICUT • LONDON

Library of Congress Cataloging-in-Publication Data

Doyle, Clar
      Raising curtains on education : drama as a site for critical
    pedagogy / Clar Doyle.
                p.   cm.—(Critical studies in education and culture series, ISSN: 1064–
      8615)
      Includes bibliographical references and index.
      ISBN 0–89789–273–9   ISBN 0–89789–274–7 (pb) alk. paper
      1. Critical pedagogy.   2. Drama in education.   I. Title.
    II. Series.
    LC196.D69   1993
    370.11'5—dc20   92–32180

British Library Cataloguing in Publication Data is available.

Library of Congress Catalog Card Number: 92–32180
ISBN: 0–89789–273–9 (hc); 0–89789–274–7 (pb)
ISSN: 1064–8615

First published in 1993

Bergin & Garvey, 88 Post Road West, Westport, CT 06881
An imprint of Greenwood Publishing Group, Inc.

Printed in the United States of America

The paper used in this book complies with the
Permanent Paper Standard issued by the National
Information Standards Organization (Z39.48–1984).

10 9 8 7 6 5 4 3 2 1

Copyright Acknowledgments

The author and publisher gratefully acknowledge permission to reprint the following
copyrighted material:

Clar Doyle, *A Site for Critical Pedagogy*. St. John's, Newfoundland: Memorial University of Newfoundland, 1989.

Clar Doyle, "A Foundation for Critical Aesthetic Education." In Amarjit and Ishmael
J. Baksh (Eds.), *Dimensions of Newfoundland Society and Education*, vol. I, 323–29.
St. John's, Newfoundland: Memorial University of Newfoundland, 1992.

For Garrett, Ceara and Damhnait

Contents

Series Foreword: Critical Pedagogy and the Politics of Performance

I contend that consciousness, while undeniably critical, is not enough to move people into the political arena. There is a political heart, more than that, a political body, that must be conjoined with mind to turn social arrest to unrest and move people to the center stage of history. It has been the neglect of this body that has made worldly drama so frightening and kept people in the role of spectator rather than political actor.[1]

In *Raising Curtains on Education* Clar Doyle demonstrates a keen sense of the importance of drama as a pedagogical practice that links theory and practice, on the one hand, and the politics of representation and the body on the other. Drawing upon a vast array of work in critical pedagogy and critical theory, Doyle uses drama as a form of cultural production to enable students to utilize their bodies and minds in the service of being able to link language and experience, desire and affirmation, and knowledge and social responsibility.

By politicizing the realm of the aesthetic and the terrain of drama, Doyle astutely illustrates how the relationship between the performance and production of plays can become both the object and the subject of critical engagement. In Doyle's approach, students engage in actual plays as part of a broader attempt to understand not only themselves and their relationships with others, but also how the dynamics of power operate in the intersection of school and society. But Doyle is not content to merely rely on a pedagogy of deconstruction, he is equally concerned that students write plays as part of a larger pedagogical process of asserting their sense of agency and their complex connections with daily life.

Doyle recognizes that dominating pedagogical practices aggressively assert the politics of the representation by positioning students as spectators rather than actors; as those who watch rather than political actors engaged in critical acts of cultural production; as witnesses rather than as human agents who write and tell their own stories. But for Doyle, it is not enough to simply reverse the binarism between witnessing and testifying, passive voyeurism, and critical agency. For Doyle, it is more important to develop a pedagogy of drama that reveals what interests these roles serve, how they become institutionalized, how they are historically constructed, and how they can be resisted, undone, and rethought outside of the binarism that defines them within structures of inequality and oppression.

Doyle wants to rescue pedagogy from a narrowly rationalist stance that ignores the body as a site of investments and desire as a productively mobilizing force. He wants to use pedagogical practices organized around the production and reading of plays that enact scenes that problemize the relationship between history, identity, and power. At the same time, he is keenly aware of deepening the possibilities of an aesthetic that is at once critical, political, and emancipatory. For Doyle, drama becomes a site where critical pedagogy comes alive; that is, it offers an opportunity to employ the critical categories of voice, difference, and community in ways that integrate the dialectical relationship between affective and rational investments, individual experiences, and the collective stories that mark out our sense of place, culture, and community. In Doyle's terms, drama becomes the dwelling place in which identities can affirm their differences, students can speak from the diverse locations of their own histories, and strive to engage their desires within rather than outside of the movement of the body, creative expression, and the language of theory.

What makes Doyle's work on drama and education so compelling is that he refuses to separate pedagogy from politics and aesthetics from the wider configurations of ideology and power. Yet, he does not reduce aesthetics or drama to a doctrinal perspective in which a pedagogy of drama collapses into either a particular ideology or reductionistic moralizing. On the contrary, Doyle wants to link pedagogy and drama to the possibilities for human agency, the power of collective struggle, and the dreams and hopes that allow students to think and act otherwise. Drama and pedagogy for Doyle are inextricably informed by an ethical discourse, one that reveals how the body is disciplined, how identity is constructed, and how subject positions are inscribed within the play of domination, power, and agency.

What is so unique about Doyle's integration of drama and critical pedagogy is his insistence that the body is more than a site of repression, more than an object shaped by the instrumental discourses of dominating pedagogical practices. Doyle wants to refashion the body as a site of desire, resistance, and possibility, one rooted in cultural politics that links thinking and feeling, understanding and compassion, and thought and affect. Desire in this approach is no longer the privileged discourse of psychoanalysis, it now becomes a central pedagogical category for understanding how students make certain investments, what moves them, and how they can use their own desires to further understand the processes by which they might become both the subject and object of history.

Clar Doyle's book will be of enormous value to teachers and other cultural workers who are interested in pedagogy as cultural politics, who value interdisciplinary approaches that connect the body and consciousness as a site of resistance and hope. This is an important book for those educators interested in how theory and practice come together to empower both teachers and students while striving to transform wider structures of domination. It is a book about the intersection of plays, texts, and bodies, one that offers teachers, students, and other cultural workers a new language for transgressing and creating borders where a multiplicity of voices can, as Doyle argues, "examine how the power at work in plays is also at work in their lives."

NOTE

1. Randy Martin, *Performance as Political Act: The Embodied Self* (Westport, Conn.: Bergin & Garvey, 1990), 1.

Henry A. Giroux

Preface

The work in this text represents an effort to put my own teaching, directing, and reflection into some form. It is always a challenge to see how our own practice stands the test of even our own articulation. Part of this exercise has to do with the "teacher question" of why I do a given thing in my teaching and the companion question of what value that thing has. We all have different answers for such questions. Then again, part of the struggle has to do with refining the questions.

While I was working on chapter five of this text I was offered a dramatic and powerful image by my daughters. The previous day one of their friends died as the result of a gunshot wound. That night hundreds of school friends and some teachers had gathered on a beach near his home and lit a massive bonfire. The bonfire was their tribute to him. It was their way of saying he was present. It was their ritual. In many ways that ritual put the work of this text into focus for me.

We all struggle to make meaning for ourselves. For sixteen years I worked with high school students, and for as many years I tried to make meaning out of what I did. I always knew there had to be more to education than telling the students what I had learned in school. I also realized that the most successful students were the ones most like the teachers. I believe now that a lot of my meaning-making was by way of reaction to educational callings as well as schooling restrictions. Some time ago I met Henry Giroux and he helped give a critical theoretical framework to my attempts at meaning-making. I have been working with these given categories, concepts, and notions for the past ten years.

Part of what we do as teachers is to try to understand our students. We try to do this so we can help them be their own best selves. In the final analysis what we do is help them help themselves. We help them to empower themselves. The more time I spend with students, both at high school and at university, the more I realize that the best gift we can give them is the gift of confidence. In order to do this we must be open, trusting, and happy to hear their voices. We need to help them examine the material and ideological world that surrounds them. Students can do this. We can help our students realize that, beginning with themselves, they are able to make a difference. They must know that they can transform. Teachers can be transformative by allowing difference and by being reflective about our own thinking and assumptions. These are some of the thoughts I have kept before me as I have written this text.

On the surface this text is about drama, but at its core it is about critical pedagogy. I am comfortable with drama and I am struggling with critical pedagogy. Every day in schools and universities we need to examine how we live out social practices that hurt as well as help people. In short we need to look at the politics of teaching. I have set realistic goals for myself in this text. I believe that critical theory, in its growing forms, offers a lucid grid for looking at education. I further believe that drama offers a viable site for a critical pedagogy. The drama I use is not exhaustive and the critical pedagogy is not complete. I am simply claiming that drama is one site for critical pedagogy.

I want to state at the outset that I have selected parts and portions of drama to serve as a site for critical pedagogy. I gleaned the landscape of drama and chose what I needed. Searching for openings that would lead me to some form of critical pedagogy, I crossed many dramatic planes and selected what I thought might be useful to my own limited agenda. This means that many key concepts and players from drama are not used in this text. This is no reflection on their worth. It is simply a measure of my critical agenda. In another way I have matched drama writers in a fashion that can only be described as strange bed-fellows. I have refused to be drawn into any of the camps that have grown up around the polarities of process drama and performance theatre. Instead I have tried to draw from both camps. As much as possible I have stayed with the drama I know. For the most part I have mentioned methods I have used in teaching and directing young people. I have referred to plays that I have worked on in some capacity or other. I have mentioned aspects of sets that I have designed or helped build. In other words I have written about the thinking and the doing that makes for praxis.

Teaching is one of the most difficult professional tasks. This burden can be lightened if we are willing to reflect on our work against the rubber wall of education. Teaching is one of the most important professional tasks. We can realize this when we think about the intellectual, moral and material power we hold with students. Teaching is one of the most political professional tasks. We can appreciate this when we admit that teachers are one of the cultural gatekeepers between school, community, and students. Teachers need all the conceptual tools available to keep all these factors balanced.

In many ways this text is driven by a series of questions having to do with teaching and learning, experience and culture, as well as with knowledge and power. Central to these clusters of questions is an overriding concern with voice. My strongest recollections about teaching in high school are found in the remembered voices of students who used drama to tell their stories. I was often amazed at the stories that were presented, in dramatic form, as if they were fiction. The enactments covered the gamut of stories about friends, mishaps, adventures, loves, and families; of loneliness, fun, horror, and happiness. Sometimes the stories left me frozen in my adjudicator's seat because I knew they were not fiction. They were an acting out of some joy or some horror that was private to the student. The student found in the drama a place to speak the truth and yet be safe. I learned a lot from those young people and their stories. I am also learning from my graduate students how drama can aid us in our struggle to make sense of the total process of curriculum development.

In the plainest terms I need to say that this text would not have been conceived or completed without the inspiration of Henry Giroux. I met Giroux at Boston University ten years ago, and he put my educational meandering in focus for he had concepts, insights, and a critical perspective. His thought and writing underpin this text.

I remain grateful to Michael Chiasson for his careful reading of the original monograph. Particular chapters of this text owe much to the critical examination they received from Andrea Rose, Dennis Mulchay, Fred Hawksley, and Barb Pepper. Their suggestions and corrections helped keep me informed and honest. I am also indebted to Amarjit Singh, Bill Kennedy, Roy Kelleher, Len Williams, and Gordon Jones for their reflection and encouragement. Nic King remains as an open invitation for me to be my best. Claire Rice and Alister Rice remain as friends. To my partners in drama, Gerry Doyle, Kevin Lewis, John Ryan, along with Pat, Mary Ellen, Jerry, Bernie, and Margaret Doyle, I am ever thankful for the yearly challenges.

I wish to thank Alice Collins, Frank Riggs, and Bob Crocker for their encouragement and material help with essential writing time. I want to thank Katherine Elliot for her direct work on this text. I owe much to the technical skill Ann Beresford brought to the completed product. Her expertize was greatly appreciated. I wish to thank Sophy Craze for her encouragement and her openness in discussing this project.

I am ever grateful for and aware of Loll Hyde-Doyle's generosity and good will.

I am deeply grateful to Rosanne Tee for her affection, patience, and shared time.

These pages, and the struggle for a critical pedagogy, are fueled by the faces of my three wonderful children.

Raising Curtains
on
Education

1

The Need for Critical Pedagogy

Sarah: For all my life I have been the creation of other people. The first thing I was able to understand was that everyone was supposed to hear but I couldn't and that was bad. Then they told me everyone was supposed to be smart but I was dumb . . . to be smart I had to become an imitation of the people who had from birth everything a person has to have to be good: ears that hear, mouth that speaks, eyes that read, brain that understands.

Mark Medoff, *Children of a Lesser God*

I begin with the premise that things can change; there is room for transformation, the process of which is brought about from within. My hope here is to aid in developing windows of transformation that can be applied to aesthetics education and to drama education in particular. This exercise will set a site for critical pedagogy. The aim is to help educators critically assess what happens in schools and to help students realize their potential in a better society. It is important to realize that there is tremendous complexity behind creating windows or sites for critical pedagogy and that such opportunities are tentative and subject to change.

In this chapter I wish to express the need for critical pedagogy and the various ideas allowing the development of particular questions that can be held up against existing and promised models in drama education. Further to this, it will be necessary to analyze the process of producing cultural forms out of lived experiences. This process, as far as drama is concerned, will be contrasted with the process of cultural reproduction. In this way we can see drama as a specific site within a culture of schooling where a form of critical pedagogy can take place.

Thomas Popkewitz (1985) wonders about the constraints to transformative education that lie within our professional institutions and situations. Unless we can somehow identify and examine these constraints, educators will always be bound by them. How can educators be helped to see that their participation can take part in changing those situations of education that are often seen as impenetrable and unalterable? This process has to do with peeling away the various levels of school life to reveal constraints and possibilities that lie beneath them. It is very easy to get trapped on the surface of schooling. After all, students must be taught; curriculum must be covered; and schools must be administered. It is often difficult to step back from this demanding work and take time to examine the levels of life that contribute to schooling. Until we can see the value of such reflection and examination, we will be restricted to mere reaction.

In recent years major studies have presented the need for encouraging, if not demanding, excellence of teaching and therefore in teacher education. The most noteworthy of these studies are *Tomorrow's Teachers* (1986) from the Holmes Group, *A Nation Prepared* (1986) by the Carnegie Task Force, and *Teacher Education in Ontario: Current Practice and Options for the Future* (1987). These documents, and many others, have been examined in great detail in other publications (Singh 1991; McLaren 1989). These, in concert with many educational publications, speak to the need for teachers who are reflective, critical, and inquiring. Teachers must be able to stand back from their own teaching and move beyond the mere execution of classroom skills and the delivery of discipline content.

Much of the literature on critical pedagogy claims that the goals of teacher education programs are often at variance with the goals of schools. Schools often want teachers who can integrate theory and practice, analyze critically, and implement change (Hopkins 1980). Teachers need to have critical insight into their roles in schools. They need to examine critically the value of the knowledge they teach and the function of schooling in general in society. A lot is expected from teachers who must be all things to all students.

David Kirk (1986) claims that teachers generally are not always prepared to face the critical issues before them and need help from all quarters: from teacher educators, from curriculum developers, and from educational administrators. How can educators help each other identify and embrace these basic concerns? Henry Giroux (1981) states that the normative interests behind educational practice must be illuminated. This becomes possible with a critical theoretical perspective that better equips educators to consider the source, meaning, and rationality behind pedagogical practice.

CRITICAL PEDAGOGY

A critical pedagogy is one in which teachers act as intelligent practitioners capable of reflective thought and take responsibility for their own professional development (Freire 1981). A critical pedagogy realizes that education is not a neutral process and that teaching methods cannot be denuded of the social, human, and historical elements that make up this process. This philosophy is difficult to put into practice. Society expects schools to correct social inequalities and reproduce the given society. Such expectations often leave the teacher in the middle of conflicting demands. In addition, a teacher has little chance of remedying a situation that is often related to complex issues of social class, cultural background, and the institutional biases of schooling (Popkewitz 1985).

Nonetheless, all teachers must be critically aware of these complex issues and realize how teachers fit into the total process.

A critical pedagogy is needed if teachers are to manage the complex social system of the classroom and diagnose the needs of individual students. As the position paper *Teacher Education in Ontario* (1987) proposes, society needs teachers who see the transmission of knowledge and culture as a foundation on which they build, not the end to which they strive. In many ways this remains a basic quest for schooling. In a society that demands that students "know things" it is difficult for teachers to struggle beyond transmission of facts to transformation. In fact, much of the curriculum that allows transformation is not of high value in schools. As Giroux (1991) proposes, it is necessary to create new forms of knowledge if we are to leave openings for transformation. How can teachers be helped to move beyond technical mastery in the classroom and toward an awareness of the deeper dimensions of education? Also, how can teachers be encouraged to examine critically the entrenched assumptions of schooling?

Emancipation, as Kirk (1986) states, lies at the heart of critical pedagogy and begins with the teacher. If teachers are able to view their practice critically and see how it merges with the culture and expectations of the institutions in which they work, then we can hope to contribute to a critical pedagogy. In the process of learning to be critical, we encounter the singular difficulty of realizing the complexities of the educational process. These complexities must be viewed through various lenses that invite us to look at the traditions (Popkewitz 1988) passed on in schools, the curricula used to reproduce these selected traditions, and the administrative and classroom management techniques used to secure such traditions. We have to remember that these traditions are often seen as sacred and treated as immutable. The traditions that underpin our schooling are rarely examined because for the most part, teachers are not encouraged to be analytical and time is rarely given for such a reflective process. The educator searching for the cracks, in the total process of schooling would benefit from a critical pedagogy.

How must educators see schooling in a way that allows for the pursuit of a critical pedagogy? How can teachers and students better appreciate that the culture of schooling is not simply a "single, unified set of patterns" (Quantz and O'Connor 1988)? The day is gone when we can approach the school as if it is simply a place for learning. Schools, the results of complex social, historical, and cultural interactions, can no longer operate as if they were gaping monoliths spurning out objective information. Schools are living places for the tangled web of humanity.

One of the crucial roles of a critical pedagogy is to help in the understanding of such tangled webs in ways that will allow both student and teacher to be transformative. As Peter McLaren (1989) claims, we should aim at providing critical categories that will allow educators to analyze schools as to the type and orientation of the transmitted knowledge, attitudes, and skills. Because we participate in the schooling process, we can come to know it as it really operates. We need to see schooling for both the impediments and the possibilities . . . for the damage and the promise. How can educators realize their potential as agents for transformation? How can we all grasp the contradictions in schooling as potential cracks, windows, or sites for developing a critical pedagogy?

What are some of the concerns that underpin the need for a critical pedagogy? It seems that many of these concerns can be placed in the form of questions. Paulo Freire and Henry Giroux write in an introduction to *Critical Pedagogy and Cultural Power* that the basis for any critical pedagogy lies in the very act of asking new questions and indicating new connections (Livingstone 1987). Giroux (1989) claims elsewhere it is essential for us to question the social and cultural control that is operational in schools and that educators must be aware of the wider social forces at work in schools. Educators have to realize that the language, resources, and practices of schools are politically burdened. The challenge is to capitalize on the political nature of schooling so that we empower people, teachers as well as learners, to take control of their own growth and transformation. We cannot do this until we understand how more fully "human experiences are produced, contested, and legitimated within the dynamics of everyday classroom life" (p. 133).

The isolation of a student's desk, in an isolated classroom, in an isolated school building, is the image of a lie. This does not mean that a student cannot feel lonely in such a desk but that such a student always connects to a larger society. In the same way, the teacher closing a classroom door does not shut out the social, cultural, or historical realities of students. Drama in education, for example, would wish to make use of such social, cultural, and historical realities by helping students understand "who they are as part of a wider social formation" (Giroux 1989, 145). Giroux states also that we need to see youth as an oppressed social category. Educators become uncomfortable when forced to look at the nature of the oppression. Yet, educators need then to look at the "'marks of cultural oppression" (Wren 1977) and examine how they contribute to or minimize that oppression. We must come to realize that terms like "oppression" and "domination" are words we need not fear. The reality embedded in these terms is at work in our daily lives. Oppression, subtle and hidden, is often of our own making. Therefore, we need to make the link between cultural oppression and economic or political domination.

Drama can help educators make such links or at least allow them to examine how one form of domination feeds on the other. When we make plays we do make such links.

How can schooling be seen as part of a wider process of education? It is important for educators to realize that schooling does not happen within a cultural fortress. Like Freire (1985) it is crucial we remember that schools represent only one site where education takes place. The forces from other social spheres walk through the school doors with the students. Drama, in particular, weaves its forceful way through the domains represented by school culture, popular culture, and class culture.

How can subjectivity and experience be given a stronger stance within the discourse of schooling? As Stanley Aronowitz and Henry Giroux (1985) point out there is a tendency to remove both teachers and students from their histories and cultural experiences.

Curriculum and methodology designed from a distance cannot take into account the historical or cultural context of either the student or the teacher. Product then comes before process, and transmission before transformation. This notion provides argument for a model of curriculum development that does not separate analysis, design, implementation, and evaluation. However, it is vital for educators to realize that who is learning precedes what is learned. It is equally essential that educators appreciate "what histories are in place" before any learning is attempted (Livingstone 1987, xv). Here is an opening for teachers to treat their students as critical agents and build on their collective histories and cultures. In other words, teachers help students develop keys to their own transformation.

Just as importantly, a teacher can let students participate in transformation and appreciate the power of their own knowledge. Teachers must give opportunities to test that power in real or fictional arenas. Here again drama can help by being that place where the real and the fictional meld together and by allowing protected sites for transformative learning.

What is the relationship between knowledge and power? Educators need to understand the power built into their own knowledge and to see how that power translates in their interactions with students and administrators. Very often educators act as if they are powerless. At other times power is used in ways that can be unknown to us because as educators we have the power of language and culture at our fingertips. We often toss this power around with great abandon. Aronowitz and Giroux (1985) claim that strategies need to be developed to identify, invigilate, and overcome the patterns of domination built into schooling.

What are the politics of cultural production and reproduction? Educators often act as if schooling is socially and politically neutral (Beyer 1980). Clearly there is a fundamental connection between what is selected for transmission within a culture and various forms of domination (Williams 1982). Teachers have to be able to realize what is hidden in the knowledge they produce and reproduce. Education has the power to mystify itself and conceal its power relationships (Willis 1981). It is very easy to simply follow the curriculum and miss the more subtle messages going out to students.

What are the discrepancies between dominant versions of reality and the lived experience of subordinate groups? Teachers have to examine their own view of reality against the real lives of their students. Teachers and students need to accept each other's reality and explore how knowledge can be produced from that acceptance. Schools must be seen as places where both teacher and student grow. Critical theories, according to John Reynolds and Malcolm Skilbeck (1976), enable people to understand their situation and appreciate the underlying social structures and power relationships. Teachers can move beyond mere interpretation and hope to influence social forces.

It is not easy for educators to examine their living in a critical sense because they take so much for granted. As the Irish poet Seamus Heaney (1987) said, "Our unspoken assumptions have the force of revelation" (p. 19). Stuart Bennett (1984) claims the taken-for-granted nature of things permeates our consciousness. He goes on to talk about how the social organization of some groups into a marginal position in society affects the young, the old, working-class people as well as those from certain ethnic backgrounds. Many students, it is true, live out their lives in cultural forms that are excluded from our school ways. The language, attitudes, mores, and hopes of home and street, are not always consistent with those found in school. Students make their own culture, which they express through dress, music, and lifestyle. The important point for educators is to realize the students are the agents of their own cultural production. Advocates of drama in a critical pedagogy would want to be in on such cultural production not only as directors but also as contributing participants.

One of the initial tasks for teachers will be to examine the "social distance" between themselves and their students. The question of social distance is a crucial one for teachers who use drama in education. This is not an easy question for teachers who realize that classroom management is bound up with social distance.

Few teachers would deny that they often use social distance as a mean to control classes. But Linda McNeil (1986) in her book *Contradictions of Control* states that schools are not simple places and facile answers for teachers will not serve the promise of a critical pedagogy.

To develop drama as a site for critical pedagogy, we must remember the reality of teachers' work. The reality of opposing curricula, demanding administrators, special students, as well as the constraints of time and space must be considered. A critical pedagogy must find ways of empowering teachers not simply blaming them. In short, the language of possibility must precede the language of critique. Teaching is a complex process. As Rex Gibson (1986) points out, teachers are both "in authority" and "an authority" (p. 17). Yet a critical theory of pedagogy can help teachers look at their practices in a fashion that will allow them to transform their work with students. Drama, I believe, can help break down some of the real barriers to transformative teaching and learning by opening fresh ways of "going about" the process of schooling. One of these ways has to do with helping students find their voices and with encouraging teachers to trade in voices of domination for voices of encouragement and empowerment. Very often this means listening to ourselves and examining what is behind our words rather than shifting language.

How can we learn to see and examine the ideology behind knowledge and culture? Michel Foucault (1980) encourages us to ask what "codes of culture" are operational in a society at any given time. Students can only be critical learners if they are able to examine coherently the belief systems that predate and predetermine their knowledge. Teachers need to come to the belief that work with students is to be transformative rather than reproductive (Quantz and O'Connor 1988).

How do teachers produce a critical dialogue that will aid in their own empowerment? It is crucial that teachers help each other become empowered individuals. Giroux (1988) writes passionately of the need for this teacher empowerment. In many ways we expect teachers to give a student what they do not have themselves:

a distinctive voice. Teachers need to be able to speak through their own needs to achieve intellectual control of their work.

How can teachers become involved in both the conception and execution of school work? Teachers must ask to do more than simply implement programs designed by others. The notion of separation of concept and execution represents an industrial ideology (Aronowitz and Giroux 1985) that does a great disservice to teachers. Separation of concept and execution makes critical learning improbable. It is not easy for harried teachers to resist ready-made learning objectives along with suggested projects and packaged student questions. This resistance is essential.

How can students be seen and treated as critical agents? Students must be given responsibility for their own learning. This calls for empowered teachers who can control what they do in class and who enable students to reflect and produce their own knowledge. Students should be allowed to explore the contradictions between their schools and the larger society with a view to changing what needs to be changed as well as affirming what needs to be affirmed.

How can students appreciate the best dimensions of their own histories, experiences, and culture? Students are often put in a position where their own histories are treated as incidental and their own experiences as unimportant. When schooling becomes more instrumental (Aronowitz and Giroux 1985), students are often removed from their grounding. Students, treated as receivers of distorted curricula, suffer the disempowerment built directly into the system.

How can students' school culture better match their class and popular culture? It is important to remember that students, like teachers, are formed out of "complex interactions" (Giroux 1984) and they cannot be treated in any monolithic pattern. Wilfred Martin (1985) sees school culture as a "multiplicity of overlapping, convergent, but also separate and divergent, values, social norms, rituals and ceremonies" (p. 3). It is within this complexity that a critical pedagogy can be developed. If critical pedagogy is to be effective it must start with students' culture. Where else would we start? Yet we must not simply use student culture to teach our own agendas. Student culture has to be seen as having value in and of itself. Teachers have opportunities in their classrooms, even within a restrictive curriculum, to build on the matches between the various cultures of students. Too much time is spent in school for educators to treat it as simply a place to go. If teachers and students are enabled to look deeply at everyday life, there is hope for a critical pedagogy. Students and teachers must be urged to value the "cultural capital" of all school members, to learn from as well as to build on that diversity.

These are only some of the questions that call for the fuller development of a critical pedagogy. It is my contention that such critical pedagogy is best developed in particular sites. Given teachers and students, working within the constraints of their own school cultures and learning endeavors, can develop an oasis of critical pedagogy. Drama is one such site.

If educators are to help in the process of creating a critical pedagogy, they have to get beyond the notion of drama as "a place of amusement only" (Goldman 1987, 2). Drama, like much of art, must be seen as speaking a language of human reality and therefore of human possibility. The notion that drama is something written by a genius for the entertainment of the few is very limiting. There is no real harm in drama as entertainment as long as its other potential is appreciated and used. Drama can be a scalpel to society and in this way serves as a powerful educational tool. Because drama has the use of word, sound, and image it can navigate social terrains with a certain amount of ease. Drama, with these words, sounds, and images can point, gesture, complain, and promise. Drama can let the right hand know what the left hand is doing. It can cut away at our rituals and institutions and expose memories and promise.

As John O'Toole (1976) said over a decade ago, educational process needs an altered vision that demands a new relationship between the school and the learner. O'Toole goes on to talk about the ways drama teachers can build on students real or invented experience. Drama can help the overall educational process by "changing the social conditions of the learning situation" (p. 54).

Drama can do much to examine attitudes and create awareness of existing relationships between people and their social institutions. For Madeline Grumet (1980) education provides a protocol that permits us to negotiate the passage of political, economic, cultural, and sexual power from one generation to another. This protocol is never neutral and drama is a firm place in which to influence the necessary negotiation. Negotiation itself is a real sign of empowerment; empowerment for both teacher and student. Educators have to look to the experiences of teachers as well as students. The learning process cannot be understood unless teachers and students contribute. Teachers should treat themselves as unfinished and not limit themselves to simply working on students. Possibly our whole notion of master teacher hurts the process of transformative education. The very notion of seeing ourselves as master teachers puts constraints on our interaction with students. With such an understanding it is difficult to know (and be willing to admit) that we need to learn along with our students. In transformative education teachers need to be able to hold back their knowledge, to let students produce their own knowledge. Teachers, like students, have multiple subjectivities (Weiler 1988) and these interactive subjectivities greatly influence the process of schooling.

Much of this text has to do with cultural production and how such a process must grow out of life and the experiences of both students and teachers. In particular I will look at what people are doing when they produce their own drama. I hope to indicate between language, location, and history the essential links that exist in forming a culture. Part of the premise at work here is the notion that who is learning precedes what is learned. People produce drama not out of inspiration alone but rather out of reflective living.

CRITICAL THEORY

If a site for critical pedagogy is to be developed, it then must be grounded in a secure critical theory. The Frankfurt School and its critical theory could help us to develop a site for critical pedagogy.

What is critical theory and where are its origins? To answer these questions it is necessary to examine the rise of the Frankfurt School as well as the development of critical theory. The intention is to expand on the ideas put forward by the Frankfurt School members and to help point the way to the positive place of human agency in the process of schooling. If sites for critical pedagogy are to be uncovered, human agency must build on the power of critique. Otherwise, both the human agency and the critique remain impotent.

At the outset it seems prudent to be aware of three terms of reference associated with this topic: critical theory, the Frankfurt School, and the Institute of Social Research. These three terms are not interchangeable and their particular relationship to each other will emerge in the following pages.

In 1923, with a large endowment from Felix Weil, the Institute of Social Research was formed in Frankfurt, Germany. David Held (1980) makes a useful distinction between the Frankfurt School and the Institute of Social Research. Held reserves the term Frankfurt School for in inner circle composed of Max Horkheimer, Theodor Adorno, Herbert Marcuse, Leo Lowenthal, and Frederick Pollock. The Institute of Social Research encompasses many other scholars and researchers who cannot be viewed as compromising a school of thought. This text concerns itself with that limited edition of the Institute of Social Research, the Frankfurt School. The thinking of the larger institute is indicated in the inaugural address of its first director, Carl Grundberg, who stressed the fact that he did not agree with the then current emphasis on university teaching at the expense of research. This early orientation was to mark the work of the larger group through the decades. However it was later, with Max Horkheimer, that the typical ideas of the Frankfurt School began to emerge. As director of the Institute, Horkheimer gathered around him a diverse group of talented thinkers and writers. Horkheimer sought to develop a group that represented varied disciplines, notably economics, psychology, history, and philosophy. For ten years the group worked out of the Institute in Frankfurt but when the Nazis assumed power in 1933, it was forced to disperse, eventually to regroup in Geneva. In 1934 a formal offer was made by Columbia University to Max Horkheimer to reestablish the Institute in New York. Following a serious reevaluation of goals and structural modifications the Institute's work continued in North America. In 1953 the Institute returned to Frankfurt (Giroux 1983).

The label preferred by the Frankfurt School for its views was critical theory. The name critical theory gives a strong indication of the intent of the Frankfurt School. Critical theory defies rigid definition and aspect-by-aspect analysis. In the same way critical theory does not purport to establish rigid philosophical structures (Jay 1973). The members of the Frankfurt School sought a process that was essentially open-ended, probing, and ongoing; this process leaves room for the social and historical moment. Critical theory does not form a unity and does not mean the same thing to all its proponents. This is in keeping with the diverse background of its members and the varied subject matter with which they dealt. This understood, we still may find in the work of Max Horkheimer, Theodor Adorno, and Herbert Marcuse the core of critical theory and its particular relevance to the critical needs of education. We should, however, keep in mind Horkheimer's warning that there can be no formula that lays down a once-and-for-all relationship between the individual, society, and nature.

Critical theory can help educators formulate and ask salient questions about schooling. If teachers are to be reflective, critical, and inquiring, then their understandings of critical analysis needs to be developed. In spite of itself, the Frankfurt School members have contributed much to a language of possibility which, however reticent, has been explored and enhanced by later critical educational thinkers. The language continues to grow. The Frankfurt School members also contributed to the idea that cultural production could be extended beyond the entertainment sphere and be situated in daily life. This idea is crucial for my text. The intent here is to indicate the power and possibility of cultural production through the medium of drama. If students can build on their own histories and experiences to produce drama then critique and emancipation are possible. Students must be helped to realize that resistance, even if quiet and subtle, is essential.

As Aronowitz and Giroux (1985) point out, the domination of knowledge is not complete and there are cracks of resistance and rainbows of imagination. In short, critical theory has left a legacy of concepts, assertions, and questions that can inform education. The following section examines briefly some of these ideas.

The critical thinking of the Frankfurt School creates a basis wherein we can perceive the individual within the complex interactions of history in a social milieu, and the personal and private experiences the individual brings to that milieu (Giroux 1983). The importance of this concept becomes stronger when we ask, within the context of schooling, whose notion of society and individuality is accepted (Popkewitz 1985).

Critical theory claims that culture can have its own capital. Yet schools presume the cultural capital (language, knowledge, taste, and aesthetic awareness) of the middle class to be natural and proceed as if all children have equal access to that specific cultural capital (Bourdieu and Passeron 1977). It is particularly crucial for us to realize that our reproduced culture is a process of deliberate continuity that represents a selected sifting (Williams 1982). It is equally crucial to acknowledge that the selected sifting is done by those who have the power to sift. This is simply to admit that the sifting is done by agents who have agendas and vested interests. The questions that must be continually asked in education is who does the sifting? For whom is the sifting done and for what reason?

It is important for educators to remember also that culture is complex. The complexity of culture is found not only in various traditions, institutions, and formations but in the dynamic interrelations that produced them. Culture cannot be seen as freefloating or independent from society. The view of culture as the expression of human consciousness shaped by daily living allows for the possibility of human agency in the meaning-making of a culture (Bennett 1981). This idea has such a wide application across the curriculum that it should be seen as central to the needs of education. In spite of this, education continues to offer to prospective teachers and students a world that is taken as being one of ready-made customs, traditions, and order.

Critical theory is needed. First, it does much to disarm the notion that the facts of school knowledge are value-free, neutral, and objective. Second, it would place behind school knowledge the necessary qualifiers of relativity and subjectivity. Next, it seeks to expose the social construction of school knowledge and operational procedures (Gibson 1986). Finally, critical theory would further point to the place of human agency in education and to the possibility of change (Marcuse 1968).

Critical theory lays a foundation for a dialectical way of thinking about schooling that stresses the historical perspective as well as the personal experience (Giroux 1983). The process of personal, social, and political emancipation must lie at the heart of any proposed critical pedagogy. Prospective teachers should be able to relate the historical knowledge gained through the teacher education process to their own personal history. In this way a teacher can hope to operate as an intelligent practitioner, capable of reflective self-development with some real understanding of the complexities of schooling. Aronowitz and Giroux (1985) are quick to point out that hidden in the complexities of schooling are not only dominant interests but also glimpses of emancipation. The challenge is to inspect the concrete of domination while seeking the cracks of hope in a critical pedagogy. The cracks are there, and teachers and students need to find the subtle wedges that can be slipped between proposed realities so that emancipatory possibilities may emerge.

Critical theory can aid education in the necessary task of understanding how schools function as agents of social and cultural production and reproduction. In this way educators can comprehensively question whose mores are affirmed, what values are embraced, and which culture is being reproduced. Paul Willis (1981) claims it is necessary to investigate the form of living collective cultural productions that occur on the grounds of what is inherited as well as what is imposed. These productions remain creative and active. Willis states further that these cultural productions are experienced as new by each individual and group. This means that teachers and students can be a positive part of the schooling process. Teachers can combine a critical theory with human agency, their own and their students', to produce daily experiences that are positive and emancipatory. To do this, teachers should act in a reflective, critical, and inquiring manner toward the knowledge they receive and then dispense. This must also apply to the methodologies they are given and ultimately use in their teaching. This knowledge is not frozen and these methods are not once-and-for-all givens.

Critical theory in education takes a critical stance to existing society while realizing that the given conditions can change. Part of the challenge for critical educational theory, according to Kathleen Weiler (1988), is to explore openings for human improvement. Of course this hope is not limited to critical educational theory. However, critical theory is willing to examine the constraints and basic assumptions of education as a necessary step toward self and societal transformation. Built into this whole quest is the knowledge that we are not free; however, we need transformation as we seek emancipation. Part of the struggle is to see the relationship between society and the individual and to examine how the constraints of one impede the other. We often treat our students as if they were absolute masters of their destinies. In fact, we are tightly meshed with our cultures and society, not in a predeterministic fatalistic fashion but in a way that demands we treat each other as sometimes bound, sometimes free. One task of critical pedagogy is to help these two elements of freedom and constraint to play off each other and allow them to work out their own dialectical relationship. Peter McLaren (1989) rightly points out that a "dialectical understanding of schooling permits us to see schools as sites of both domination and liberation" (p. 166). This stance allows us to examine the world as it is and still have hope. This means we can encourage our students to confront their reality and still work on it because change is possible.

In general, critical theory seeks to understand all forms of social practice as well as the factors that hinder self-consciousness and free development. Critical theory can be used also to show that the structure of society contains unrealized potentialities. With regard to education, critical theory can help point to the inequities and injustices in schooling and examine their origins. Rex Gibson (1986) indicates that a critical theory further needs to propose remedies to the inequalities and injustices. This notwithstanding, I contend that neither simple causes nor blanket remedies can exist for these inequalities. Given that the mosaic of schooling is patched with complex interests and possibilities, promises of remedy must vary and be appropriate.

One of the great promises from critical theory and for critical pedagogy is being focused in the work of resistance writers. Foremost among these scholars are Henry Giroux and Michael Apple. These writers continue to point to the fact that cultural and social reproductions allow for moments of opposition and resistance. Students and teachers encounter this fact every day. Opposition and resistance, however, are not always driven by critical thought or even comprehension.

The final sections of this text will suggest critical invitations to resistance within the site of drama education. I hope to do this by using conceptions of culture, ideology, reproduction, and power to inform human agents working within a drama education framework how they can take advantage of critical theory to exercise a critical pedagogy. Part of the task here is to use critical theory in a grounding fashion while allowing the critical thinking of the last decade to help us put the face of possibility on schooling. There is little doubt that we have moved well beyond the gloom and doom of Frankfurt tomes. The challenge still remains to make pedagogy critical in our daily classes. At this stage I understand critical pedagogy to include the possible. Critique, although a necessary stage, is not enough. Critique allows us to measure the playing field. Possibility lies in playing while knowing what the rules are. If we know the field and understand the rules, then we can hope. Part of that hope may lie in challenging or even changing the rules, but at least we are in on the game.

There is no claim here that critical theory and the work of the Frankfurt School should be accepted in an absolute fashion. Rather, I am suggesting that this extensive and penetrating effort should not only be recognized but be seen as a practical aid to forming a critical pedagogy.

2

Aesthetics and Drama Education

Stephanie: Music, Dr. Feldmann, is the purest expression of humanity that there is. You see, there's no God, you know, Dr. Feldmann, but I know where they got the idea; they got it from music.

Tom Kempiniski, *Duet for One*

One purpose of this chapter is to lay the foundation for claiming that aesthetics has the power to help us see the world differently. In viewing a work of art, through touching a sculpture, or by experiencing drama, we can look at our lives and situations in a different way. The critical examination of artistic presentation allows us to get behind the piece itself. In this way we may be able to understand the various vested interests, agencies, and mind sets that drive our own worlds. John Dewey (1934) indicates that we should be aware of what happens to art when it has a long history or has received unquestioned admiration. He claims that the art becomes isolated from the human conditions that produced it and that when art objects are separated from their conditions of production, "a wall is built around them" (p. 3). The greater the isolation, the greater the distance from reality the less opportunity to inform. In this way, art invents mystery and works against a critical pedagogy. There is an opportunity here for us to investigate how sensitivities, tastes, and awareness are produced (Popkewitz 1988). Works of art, sculpture, music, or drama are experienced by students in relation to their own backgrounds. How can we help students obtain the skills necessary to examine their own aesthetic and social values? How can we help students realize that behind an aesthetic work may lie someone else's values? How can we, as teachers, be more open to the real message behind a student's statement that a presented aesthetic form "is stupid"? What are the students really saying? It is possible that the students are stating that the reproduced cultural expression of another class simply does not speak to them at this time and in these circumstances. I am not claiming that a rejection of an art work is necessarily an exercise in resistance in and of itself, but with critical thought it could become so. It is helpful for us to remember that art is produced and experienced socially. In that contest, critical theory can help us probe the layered meanings behind drama. A critical theory, according to Karen Hamblen (1988), can aid in the examination of the historical and subjective origins of a work of art. Hamblen states that we have to pay close attention to that which allows or denies possibilities for imagining and creating other aesthetic worlds.

ART

One of the major contributions critical pedagogy can make is that it has the possibility to demystify art. Art has often been separated from its context in a way that leaves it hovering as a cultural abstraction. Art is not above its cultural source. Very often, we give art a posture of detachment that is simply impossible. Artistic creation can only happen in a given culture. We can understand art from our own biographies and sensibilities, which are generated within a given culture. Very often pedestrians want to claim certain art forms for themselves and remove them from their cultural soil. This removal is illusionary and dishonest. A critical pedagogy would guard against such usurpation of art forms. A critical pedagogy would use such art forms for its own transformative ends to examine and to change. Artists have always held up a mirror to society; but as critical educators we need to see how such mirrors are used.

David McLellan (1979) asserts that the most impressive achievement of the Frankfurt School lay in the field of aesthetics. For the Frankfurt School art can be a protest against prevailing conditions. The meaning and function of art change with time and circumstances. Great art, what Adorno calls autonomous art, has the capacity to transform a particular, individual experience. Art, through its form, can create images of beauty and order or contradiction and dissonance.

Art is most critical when it seeks autonomy, when it negates the restraining reality of its own roots. Art music must be able to restructure conventional patterns of meaning. The most genuine forms of art are those that resist pressure to reflect societal presumptions. Art needs to be able to reformulate the relations between subjectivity and objectivity. In so doing, a successful work of art does not simply resolve contradictions in a spurious harmony, but reveals these contradictions within its own structure. Art provides a medium for critical thinking to the extent that it holds up images of life that contradict the existing reality. Art becomes false, however, if it promises Utopia through its images or suggests that Utopia can be realized in the aesthetic realm. If it is to open the established reality to alternative visions and possibilities (Jay 1973), art must retain its own freedom. This element of the Frankfurt School's critical theory will prove helpful in critiquing existing models of aesthetics, and drama education.

The Frankfurt School's sociology of art does not reduce cultural phenomena to an ideological reflex of class interests. According to Adorno (1975) the task of criticism is not so much to search for particular interest groups to assign value to cultural phenomena, but to see how powerful interests realize themselves through the cultural phenomena. Until social contradictions are reconciled in reality, art needs to maintain a negative moment. Marcuse's (1968) notion of affirmative culture is helpful in understanding what the

Frankfurt School meant by negative culture. By affirmative culture, Marcuse means the culture that calls for a segregation of the spiritual world from civilization. This independent spiritual realm is often seen to foreshadow an eternally better world that must be affirmed. This world is seen as essentially different from the world of daily living. In an affirmative culture only activities and objects, which point to this elevated and separated sphere, have value. Marcuse, alternatively assumes, that culture should reflect a concern for the individual's claim to happiness. Clearly, this claim for happiness, as presented by affirmative culture, hits a sour note in a world that for many simply means need, privation, and labor. It follows that affirmative culture cannot meet such expectations of happiness. This element of critical theory, as elaborated by Marcuse, will be important in setting a foundation for reconsidering and rethinking drama as a critical form of pedagogy.

In *An Essay on Liberation*, Marcuse (1969) writes that the aesthetic dimension can serve as a sort of gauge for a free society. In the process of human liberation Marcuse sees a new role for art. Art could become an integral factor in shaping the reality of life. As far as the Frankfurt School members were concerned, art can make the familiar unfamiliar and cast a new light on the familiar. For the Frankfurt School, art needs to shock and provoke and in a real way shake the foundations of an unequal society. Marcuse suggests that art in its autonomous state, a state guaranteed by its aesthetic form, subverts the dominant consciousness and legitimately protests given social relations. The truth of art then lies in the fact that the world really is as it appears in the work of art. In this way the inner logic of the work of art fosters another type of reason and another form of sensibility that questions the reason and sensibility embedded in dominant social institutions. Williams (1982), for example, writes of authentic naturalism in theatre where the relations of people and their environments are not only represented but actively explored.

When Marcuse writes of the aesthetic form, he is referring to the transformation of a given content into a self-contained whole that can be a novel, a poem, a sculpture, or a play. This work of art can assume a significance and truth of its own. In this way a work of art, a play for instance, can represent reality while holding it up for legitimate scrutiny. Proceeding from this, the critical function of art can be seen as residing in the aesthetic form to become a vehicle not only of recognition but of indictment. This concept can be applied to the critical dimensions of aesthetics and drama education.

It needs to be remembered that art cannot sever itself from its origins, given that the genesis of true art bears witness to the limitations of freedom and human fulfillment. It bears witness to dialectical truth. There is in art, an unbridgeable gap between subject and object, individual and society, and individual and individual. It must also be remembered that art, of itself, cannot change the world. It can, however, point to a change in consciousness in people who can then change the face of the lived experience. To work for a change of consciousness artists may have to place their work as a wedge between the people who live and the event that is lived.

Maxine Greene (1980) reminds us how the aesthetic has been treated and handled in North American schools. The aesthetic has been devalued and moved to the back burners of curriculum. Because the aesthetic serves the opposite polarity to objectivity, verifiability, and neutrality, it is often regarded as soft or invalid. Because art, in its various forms, has the audacity to challenge attitudes and institutions within society, it is treated with uneasiness and discomfort. If, however, the image is pleasing or if the play is affirming, then all is well. If however, the sculpture points or the play questions, the aesthetics police move in. Rarely do they move in with truncheons, but rather they move in with subtly; the subtly of curriculum back burners. The arts, as Greene claims, are sentimentalized and trivialized, and associated with play. There is hope that some of these attitudes and pedagogical practices are changing.

Janet Wolff (1984) is persuasive in indicating that art is a social product produced inside the lived reality. A critical sociology of the arts reveals that there are many extra-aesthetic elements involved with aesthetics education. The principal message is for us to realize that art is not above social and political consideration. Moreover, art is often manipulated for business and ideological reasons, a fact a brief tour through any T-shirt outlet will confirm.

The growth of interest in exploring the social history of art is encouraging for critical pedagogy. If students are to be helped to demystify art and find voice through art, then the social grounding of art must be interrogated. The wonder of drama for critical pedagogy, is that it is open to such interrogation. People need to probe in what manner and form they present drama to the public. It is sufficient to note how large theatre companies dictate the remounting of established plays. In short, the controlling theatre company ensures that the script, score, set, lighting, costumes, and staging are all the same. The original is simply reproduced. Certainly the new presentation is robbed of any creative possibility. This, I believe, has implications for a critical pedagogy.

ART AND IDEOLOGY

Part of the task of allowing drama its critical moment is to expose the ideological nature of art. Art is always a vexing question. The relationship between art and ideology must be seen as a dialectical one. This dialectical relationship between art and the social mentality gives power to art. If art was a mere reflection of ideology it would remain somewhat powerless, but it is not powerless. Art has the power of critique and possibility. Even though art belongs to a given ideology, it can also probe that ideology. This power needs to be guarded carefully.

In another way, art is often that link between our experience and our struggle to express that experience. Art can probe what lies behind our experience. As Adorno (1984) said, art criticizes society "just by being there" (p. 321). The notion of ideology is very useful in examining the culture of schools. As Giroux (1983) points out "ideology refers to the production, consumption, and representation of ideas and behavior, which can either distort or illuminate the nature of reality" (p. 143). Before the notion of ideology can be useful to critical pedagogy we first must strip it away from the danger zone. The term ideology has been too closely associated with particular political systems (Reynolds and Skilbeck 1976). Ideology, a feature of all societies, should not be seen as a tainted word but as a cluster of beliefs and values binding a group. The content of ideology, we must remember, includes the religious, the aesthetic, the metaphysical, the economic as well as the political touching each of us where we live.

If cultural experiences can influence ideologies at development, then it follows that an examination of given ideologies can help us understand certain cultures. The influential line between culture and ideology flows in both directions. Teachers work within ideological frameworks. Every day teachers run headlong into ideological brick walls. People with parcels of beliefs and values want the same parcels for their children and future employees. Schooling has become an open battleground for conflicting ideologies. Just as we have to see the ideological nature of school culture (Giroux 1984), we also have to realize the ideological nature of art, sculpture, music, and drama. Teachers need to see ideology as it weaves its way through school culture.

Peter McLaren (1989) says ideology refers to the way we make sense and meaning of our worlds. Without ideology we could not easily understand the world. Once we have accepted an ideology, no matter how we refer to it, we act out of that ideology. Our inherited ideologies give us frameworks or grids with which to view the world. That framework, that grid, can be both illuminating and distorting. Part of the challenge for teachers is to be able to realize how our educational thinking and practice is governed by ideology. What do we accept or expect as being common sense and natural? What forms of art make sense to us? What rituals do we see as worthwhile? What images reflect real life as we know it? What plays will we allow to speak for us?

Catherine Belsey (1980) reminds us that ideology is inscribed in specific discourses. Discourse involves certain shared assumptions that appear on the surface of our language. Therefore, part of the challenge for a critical pedagogy, in this instance, is to make the discourse of aesthetics accessible. If we are to use art to help us understand our worlds, it does not make sense to impede that process with a new cumbersome language. This is not a simple matter. Certain terms have been given specific meanings and very often we need these terms to elucidate our subjectivities. The language of aesthetics is filled with elusive terms and concepts. However, these must be used to demystify the worlds they represent, not set up new barriers. This is an awkward wire to negotiate. We need the elaborated discourse, yet we wish its use to be illuminating.

One of the things we do with art is divorce it from the process that produced it. We finish a piece of art before we show it. The group standing around a street glassblower possibly provides evidence that indicates we would like to know how things are made. If that is true, then we might also like to get behind the thinking, attitudes, values, and culture of the art maker. Then, possibly, we really can see how the art was made. Of course keeping the artistic process away from the consumer increases the mystery that creates distance. In time, it becomes difficult to connect the art with its real life grounding. In this way it becomes easy for the artist to be called "the inspired," "the creator," or "the genius." Such designations create difficulty for critical pedagogy. The face of expressed culture changes to embrace or resist other equally viable cultures. The subject is never a monolith. Nowhere is this seen more clearly than in the complex relationships between students and teachers in their various formal and informal settings. As Aronowitz and Giroux (1985) claim, education becomes a central terrain where power and politics operate out of a dialectical relationship between individuals and groups. People have to be allowed to examine the contradictions and the cracks in transmitted knowledge. They have to be encouraged to produce new creative forms. Art exists in part to help people speak for themselves. Janet Wolff (1984) points to such possibilities when she states that works of art are not closed, self-contained, or transcendent entities. I believe we often treat works of art as if they stand in isolation from the stuff of society. Wolff insists that works of art are the products of specific historical practices, representing the ideas and values of a specific group. If this is so, then the field is open for human agency not only to examine, interpret, and demystify artistic formulations but also to create new ones that bear the imprint of the agent and speak for that agent. As Landon E. Beyer (1980) asserts, art can help us see current realities and future possibilities. It can be claimed further that art holds within itself images of emancipation (Gibson 1986). That is why Frankfurt School members regarded art as having great importance in the free development of individuals and society. Art, then, is not an escape from the reality of daily living but a means to place understanding and control within that reality. It becomes equally important to remember that art can be used for liberation as well as control.

DRAMA

I now want to focus the aesthetic domain on drama as it exists in relation to education. Drama education, like aesthetic education in general, exists in forms that create, rather than explore, problems. It is my contention that a critical theory of drama does not currently exist in a fashion that does justice to the possibilities of drama education. Elliot Eisner's (1979) allegation, that the absence of aesthetic theory is more important than most people realize, still stands. A review of research on aesthetic education does little to belie Eisner's original position (Wittrock 1986). Moreover, aesthetic theory is given little prominence in most teacher training programs. Yet, as we have seen, aesthetics offers a fundamental way of looking at the world. What is true for aesthetics on the whole is true for drama. As we read in *Postmodernism, Feminism, and Cultural Politics* (Giroux, ed. 1991) it is necessary to begin learning how to read the aesthetic images that surround us. This becomes a crucial point if we are considering the use of aesthetic images as raw material for dramatic production. Drama is symbolic in its medium and its process. The very process of drama is often symbolic. We use symbols to convey meanings that might be beyond words. Often in drama we use symbolic movement, light, and properties to emphasize or contradict the spoken word. This practice indicates the power of drama.

The challenge for a critical pedagogy is to learn to read such symbols critically. We need to be better able to learn the meanings behind our symbols so we can use them for our own empowerment. Such symbols can be used as keys to help students unlock the culture in which they find themselves. Symbols can be used to mystify or to liberate. Transformative education would want to use cultural symbols to liberate. Drama offers many opportunities to examine cultural symbols and put them in the hands of students.

As indicated above, one of the challenges of critical pedagogy is to help teachers examine the common sense assumptions of schooling, thinking, and practices. This challenge is to realize how school practices are elevated to the status of ritual. One other particular challenge is to appreciate how the arts become part of those ritualistic practices. The arts are a fertile ground for a critical discussion of schooling. In many ways painting, music, and drama can be seen as outside of the constrains of other school subjects. Yet the arts are subject to the administrative, economic, and political realities of schooling.

One of the great contributions of critical theory to aesthetic analysis is in its insistence that art must be seen as growing out of particular social contexts (Gibson 1986). The value of suggesting drama as a site for critical pedagogy lies in the possibility of enlarging the social grounding of art. In this way, particular biographies and cultural experiences can be seen as fruitful material for drama production. Furthermore, the notion of art being grounded in society gives critical pedagogy a powerful tool to examine plays suggested for school use. Such plays can be scrutinized for the ideologies that support them. What values, beliefs, and relationships are being depicted or taken for granted? What symbols and images are being used for what purpose? What cultures are being affirmed or ridiculed? Whose truth is here? Such questions allow us to see the possibility of emancipatory activity through art and drama.

A critical pedagogy would not allow culture's art to be removed from students. Certain cultural art and artifacts have been made the property of the influential, namely those who have the status, prestige, and capital to capture it. This private ownership of art, in its many forms, removes these cultural expressions from their base. In actuality art forms are often used to disenfranchise both teachers and students. If I don't appreciate, accept, and affirm certain art in a certain way, then somehow I am less. It is very possible that I might appreciate, accept, or affirm in my own way. In reality art can have value for me even if I reject it. It might speak to me of another reality, one I do not wish to affirm. I may wish to distance myself from the foundations of inequality that are represented in a given art form. On the other hand, I may wish to distance myself from the manner in which an art form is used further to isolate it from its grounding and potential meaning.

As Maxine Greene (1990) suggests, art can help us open up situations that require investigation and interpretation. In a critical pedagogy we need to explore the real nature of art and, as Wolff (1984) claims, demystify the ideas that maintain the autonomy and universal quality of works of art. Wolff would want us to be aware of the extra-aesthetic factors that sneak into our understanding of art. This is where some appreciation of the place ideology plays in art can help to inform critical pedagogy. We cannot understand art outside our own constructs of reality nor can we understand art outside the material conditions of the artist. In a simplistic sense, we put into art what we know thereby acting out our own reality. This acting out is literally true in drama.

Drama has a long and ambiguous history in education. Drama within the process of schooling, has its own philosophies, aims, and practices. To help redeem drama education from the constraining powers of absolute definitions of knowledge and activities (Bates 1981) it will be necessary to examine its philosophies, aims, and practices from a critical perspective. It will also be necessary to probe the relationship between drama and society. Only within that relationship can the role of drama be seen as a transformative force.

David Hornbrook (1989) operates from the premise that drama belongs at the center of the arts curriculum. His struggle is to illuminate dramatic art's place in culture and history. Hornbrook further reminds us that art and drama production can only be done "within the critical parameters of a culture" (p. 100). It is impossible to produce art outside the social and historical circumstances of the artist's life. Hornbrook, who views the relationship between art and ideology as crucial, is quick to point out that art's relationship to our understanding of the world is a complex one. This complexity can be softened if we treat the relationship between art and ideology as dialectical. In this way art bounces off ideology and vice versa. Art can distance itself from ideology and allow us to examine the given ideology. Hornbrook, building on the work of Raymond Williams, stresses that art fits that space between experience and our struggle to articulate that experience. In this way art can be reclaimed for history and culture.

The process of thinking, building on the blocks of personal histories and experiences, is enclosed in the artistic form. The sculpture, the building, the painting, the book, or the play can be seen and touched. In a sense the aesthetic is limited by its form. What is represented is bigger than what is presented. We are left with the object. Very often the subject is left behind the finished product. In order to get back to the human conditions or the subject that informed the production, we have to peel away many layers. When Dewey (1934) talks about the refined and intensified forms of art, he is referring to those forms removed from the experiences that allowed it to be produced.

Part of the agenda in later chapters will be to connect some drama productions with their foundational experiences. Plays will be looked at, not only for their artistic quality, but for the expression of their cultural groundings and the critical questions they can suggest. If we remind ourselves that paintings and plays can exist outside galleries, museums, and theatres, then we can think about the production circumstances of these art forms. In this way the art form does not have to be dead.

Every opening night play has a history of reflection, discussion, writing, and rehearsal. Every play has a collective past, one that includes not only a playwright but director, designer, technician, publicist, and of course actors. Each person brings a past and a power to the script. When each person is finished with the script it is not the same as when the playwright first submitted it. Just as the script was influenced by agenda, resources, and time, so is the presented play. Change any one circumstance of the scripting or any one person in the collective, the product will be different. This logic shows the power of the process. Art cannot be removed from the interests of life. Wolff's concept that the nature of art is a work of "located production" is most helpful here (1984, 137). This perception allows us to explore the groundings of cultural productions, plays for example, in ways that illuminate realities and transformative possibilities. The traditional notion of artist as creator is less helpful in understanding the reality of cultural production. This notion points to an unreality about art and nudges us to pass by. We can ignore such art because "it has nothing to do with us."

If we are to look at things in new ways and search for windows of transformation, then we have to put emphasis on the critical and allow analysis of what is given. Greene (1990) is helpful when she reminds us that critical understanding precedes freedom. Part of this understanding lies in our remembering that our lives are in common with other people and that our cultural productions grow out of our sharing with others. Cultural productions are not pulled out of the air. As Greene states, "to be aware of authorship is to be aware of situationally and the relation between the ways in which one interprets one's situation and the possibilities of action and choice" (p. 23).

CULTURAL FOUNDATIONS OF DRAMA

For the Frankfurt School, especially Horkheimer, Adorno, and Marcuse, sociology and critique are inseparable. In order to critique art, or a particular cultural artifact, it is necessary to understand that work in its social origins and to be aware of its form, content, and function in terms of the total society. Art does not exist out of context and should not exist in isolation. Society expresses itself through its cultural life, and these expressions contain references to the social totality. During their association with the Institute of Social Research, Adorno, Horkheimer, Marcuse, Lowenthal, and Walter Benjamin all were concerned with aesthetic theory and the critique of culture. As far as Horkheimer was concerned, a theory of culture must make reference to the processes of production, reproduction, distribution, exchange, and consumption (Held 1980).

If a notion of culture is to be useful to this text, some questions need to be asked. First, is culture to be understood as the arts, as a system of meanings, attitudes, and values or as a way of life? The notion of culture is complex. Our everyday use of the term indicates this complexity. We speak of going to a new culture, having a cultural evening, and of something that is part of our culture. Culture is not free floating but is the expression of human consciousness, which is shaped by social living. This view of culture (Bennett 1981) allows for the possibility of human agency in the meaning-making of a culture. Peter McLaren (1989) uses the term "to signify the particular ways in which a social group lives out and makes sense of its given circumstances and conditions of life" (p. 171). It is within such a concept of culture that people are able to seek their own voices through the construction of a language of possibility (Giroux 1988). Culture develops as we find ways of sharing and articulating our experiences. This sharing and articulation are the material of drama. If a critical pedagogy of drama is to be developed, then it will be necessary to expand the use of cultural symbols. In other words, we can give power to teachers and students by helping them better understand and use cultural symbols.

As far as the Frankfurt School members were concerned, culture could not be understood only in terms of itself and, therefore, could not be seen as independent from society. For these theoreticians, culture stemming from the organizational basis of society is represented in the form of ideas, norms, and artistic expressions. In short, culture is the offspring of intelligence and art. Marcuse makes a distinction between material and intellectual culture. By material culture Marcuse means the daily patterns observed in behavior and operational values as well as the social, psychological, and moral dimensions of family, leisure, education, and work. By intellectual culture he means the values of science, humanities, art, and religion. This distinction will be useful in any critical discussion of aesthetics and drama education.

For Adorno and Horkheimer (1972) culture was seen as a crucial moment in the development of historical experience and everyday life. These writers claimed that the substance of culture resides in the material life process. This is not to claim that culture represents a simple correspondence to the economic sphere; yet it is easy to see how the notion of culture as an open, living, changing, growing, freeing process could be lost if seen in a frozen fashion (Giroux 1982). We must remember that various cultures have within them contradictions and, therefore, opportunities for transformation.

Adorno and Horkheimer first used the term "culture industry" in *Dialectics of Enlightenment* (1972). They chose this term over "mass culture" because they wished to examine the process that fused the old and the familiar into a new quality. Philip McCann's (1988) idea of inventing tradition is most helpful. McCann examines social and cultural identities so that beliefs and presuppositions, originating from certain dominant groups, are accepted as normal, natural, unquestionable, and transcendent. Popkewitz (1988) hints that aesthetics represent elite sections of society. Within such a process, Popkewitz suggests, it is easy for us to get caught up with the reproduction of specific sensitivities, values, and awareness.

It seems prudent at this stage to state that the expression *cultural industry* is not to be taken literally but refers to the standarization of culture itself and the process of its distribution, though not the actual production process. However, the formulas that are used for the mass production of songs, books, and plays would seem to indicate that the industry reaches the production process. The work of David Livingstone (1987) and his colleagues is informative in this light when they discuss the place of mass-media in popular culture.

Adorno's (1975) claims that the culture industry needs to be taken seriously, not in the way it takes itself seriously, but in the fact that the culture industry calls for serious critique. The success of the culture industry calls for mass conformism; we are asked to conform without knowing why we do so or even thinking about what we are doing. In this way, conformity can replace consciousness. As Aronowitz and Giroux (1985) point out, the culture industry is ubiquitous and through its various forms manufacturers a vision of the world. The products of the culture industry are taken to represent given and eternal truths. The real interests of the culture consumer are not taken into account. The culture industry solves conflicts only on the surface, only in appearance. The culture industry asks the consumers not to judge for themselves but to echo and live the values and attitudes of the status quo. This is made possible, as far as some Frankfurt School members are concerned, by the culture industry's use of style. A unique style may certainly add distinction to a work of art. However, in the culture industry, style can subsume the message and the content. When this is done, art cannot fulfill its promise of possibility or emancipation. It can only help escape from the realities of the present. We can be captivated by style and in its thrall will often remain critical. Style, in the hands of the culture industry, allows culture to be administered. In this light it is easy to see how the art critic becomes the mouthpiece of the status quo. It is the art critic who condemns any deviation from the accepted style and artistic norms and in so doing draws tight the rope of conformity. Those artists who do not conform do not find success.

In this fashion conformity is its own reward. Of course, many visual and performing artists do break out of the mold of a given style and therefore break with the normalization process. It is with such breaks that art can be seen as emancipatory. Breaking with the dominant expectations often calls for the price of isolation and lack of immediate success. Aesthetic education, and in particular drama education, in its effort to offer a critical form of pedagogy needs to consider the potential benefits rendered by these departures from conformity.

If this text is to speak to the real life possibility of a critical aesthetic pedagogy, then the concepts of cultural production and reproduction must be examined. We need to take seriously the impression that schools not only reproduce cultural content but that schools produce aspects of cultural content. We need to remember that cultural and economic reproductions are closely linked. It is obvious that schools reinforce these links and often operate as if such links are unbreakable. What are the implications here for critical pedagogy? The premise in this text is that critical pedagogy can help transform a particular culture. The challenge here is to appreciate the processes that allow cultural reproduction from cultural production and link these with social reproduction. To do this Paul Willis (1981) claims it is necessary to investigate the forms of lived cultural productions in terms of what is inherited as well as what is imposed. These productions still remain creative and active. Willis further states that these cultural productions are experienced as new by each individual and group. The relevance then of the concept of cultural production for this text can be seen when it is realized that educational institutions give official acceptance to a culture that may actually be the property of a dominant group. This official culture is then proclaimed as singularly legitimate and objective.

Kathleen Weiler (1988) is most helpful when she underlines the real distinction between theories of cultural production and theories of cultural reproduction. She reminds us that theories of cultural reproduction failed to relate the complexities of life or indicate the possibilities for resistance and transformation. The attempt of this text is to help point to the possibilities, within the cultural production of drama, that allow both resistance and transformation. Richard A. Quantz and Terence W. O'Connor (1988), on the other hand, encourage us to listen to both dominant and "other" voices to appreciate the complex web of cultural life. In league with that concept, this text aims to examine the possible functions of drama in a positive fashion within the contradictions and cultures of schooling. It would seem that drama, as it exists and is used in education, could be an appropriate place to play out these contradictions and examine varied cultural capital skills.

The whole idea of cultural capital is a crucial one for this text. As I noted earlier, culture includes beliefs, knowledge, customs, language, attitudes, and behavior. We all have what Pierre Bourdieu (1977) calls cultural capital. That is, we all have beliefs, knowledge, customs, language, attitudes, and behavior that are exhibited in certain forms. Because we live in a pluralistic society, manifestations of culture are hardly ever uniform or all inclusive. It follows that all manifestations of culture are not equally included, accepted, or affirmed. It also follows that one or more forms of cultural capital will be dominant, that is, favored. If that is so then it would help critical educators to be able to use the idea of cultural capital to direct their work. This point is especially valid in our dealings with young people. We have to realize how we can use this idea to understand, affirm, and build on students' culture. As Michael Apple (1985) suggests, we need to explore how schools can help produce cultural capital that tips the social scales toward possibility and transformation.

Art forms in their very elements of word, color, and tone depend on cultural material. Art shares this material with the existing society. This is true even when art speaks its own language. This might appear as a limitation of aesthetic autonomy. On the contrary, it delineates art, as a liberating factor, as an integral part of that which it seeks to change. In drama, as in other forms of art, the given reality can be distorted to speak the unspeakable. In this way, the art form can be indictment as well as celebration, depending on what emancipation is called for at the given moment. Greene (1980) claims that learners ought to be free to perceive things in their complexity, to see the possible within everyday things, and to be free to interpret possibilities hidden in the cultural tradition.

If drama is to have a critical moment, its users must have a balanced sense of the place of aesthetics. The world intended in a play script, or any art form, is never simply the given world of everyday life. Yet it is not mere illusion. We have already determined that the elements that go into the art form are elements of the real world. The art form, however, is a fictitious reality. In the aesthetic formation, things appear not only as they are but as they can be.

Critical theory seeks to understand all forms of social practice and the factors that hinder self-consciousness and free development. Critical theory further seeks to show that the structure of society contains unrealized potential. The Frankfurt School's analysis of contemporary culture represents one of the most important areas by which we realize how dominant ideologies penetrate everyday interpretative schemes (Held 1980).

So far the search in this text has been for elements of critical theory that could help lay the foundation for rethinking drama as a critical form of pedagogy. These elements can be listed in a fashion that can be directly applied to drama education. As indicated earlier, critical theory offers a strong legacy that can be applied to aesthetic education. In this text, I have selected only those elements from aesthetics that have direct application to drama pedagogy. The following capsule comments on how the elements extracted from critical theory can now be used to underpin questions that can be asked of drama education.

CRITICAL QUESTIONS

Critical theory seeks to understand social factors that hinder self-consciousness and free development as well as those social factors that contain unrealized potential. If that is so, how does drama as a form of pedagogy fit the forms of social practice that hinder self-consciousness and free development? Further to this we can ask: Can drama serve in realizing society's potential?

Culture, in part, is the expression of human consciousness that is shaped by social living. Culture also has to do with the daily patterns of living, the various dimensions of leisure, education, and work as well as the values of science, humanities, art, and religion. The tools of technology, modern administration, and the rationality of domination hold sway over culture and the latter culture is objectified through the institutions of family, school, church, and workplace. How does drama, then, fit the social shaping of human consciousness? How does drama help objectify culture?

Culture can be seen to have its capital. Within much of western society possession of the correct cultural capital is necessary for participation in the dominant groups. We can rightly ask in what way is drama an indicator or transmitter of cultural capital? Whose cultural capital does drama indicate and transmit?

Cultural production occurs on the grounds of what is collectively lived, inherited, and imposed. These cultural productions are experienced as new by each individual and group. How does drama fit into the whole process of cultural capital? How does drama, within an educational institution, help make official a culture that is the property of the dominant groups?

The emancipatory effects of art are generated by the rejection of dominant forms of world order and by showing how powerful interests realize themselves through cultural phenomena. That being the case, how does drama become a vehicle not only of recognition but of indictment? Within it demystifying possibility how can drama be used for celebration as well as indictment? How can drama help break the monopoly of sociohistorical reality and point to the possibilities that are embedded in the cultural tradition?

The culture industry attempts to fuse the old and the familiar into a new quality. Built on the standardization of the thing itself (reification), the culture industry calls for the consumer to be acritical and to echo the values and attitudes of the status quo. The products of the culture industry are taken to represent given and eternal truths. How is drama used by the culture industry to replace consciousness with conformity? Further to this question, how can drama help, rather than impede, the development of autonomous, independent, and critical individuals?

One of the main tools of the culture industry is style. Style captivates, and in the face of it we often remain acritical allowing culture to be administered. Therefore, the question is how does drama allow itself fall victim to style and how is this manifest in drama's pedagogical forms?

Within critical theory there is a manifest distrust of claims to the reconciliation of contradictions. Does the particular drama form resist the temptation to resolve contradictions in a spurious harmony? Does the drama form show the contradictions of social reality in its own structure?

Art becomes false if it promises Utopia through its images or suggests that such a state can be realized in the aesthetic realm. Can drama help develop a language of possibility and help fulfill the promise of emancipation?

Affirmative art sees the entire sphere of material production as tainted by poverty, severity, and injustice and refuses any demands to protest that sphere. Autonomous art protests the given sphere and offers hope. Can drama help subvert the dominant consciousness and the ordinary experience and protest the given social relations? Can drama provide liberating images of the subordination of need, poverty, and destruction to the will to live? Can drama provide a viable example of autonomous art?

Art must intervene actively in consciousness in a formative way. If this is the case, how can drama help form a consciousness where people can change the face of lived experience?

In this chapter the elements of critical theory have been extracted and questions posed in a fashion that can be used in a critique of existing models of drama education. These elements of critical theory can further be used to point to a foundation for reconsidering and rethinking theories of critical aesthetic education as well as critical drama education.

3

Drama and Education

Michael: Ah. But you've got the solution, don't you? It's so easy. We'll just leave County Tyrone. We'll go to America. We can stay with your cousin in . . . what's it called . . . the Bronx is it? That'll be lovely. You'll be a clerk in some store and I'll be a mechanic. We'll become Americans. So what if this family's been here in County Tyrone these last thousand years. So what if this farm belonged to my Dad and his Dad before him back to Earl of Tyrone. That's no reason to fight for anything is it? It's easy. We'll go to America. There's a grand thing to do!

Christopher Humble, The Flight of the Earls

Drama has had a long and ambiguous history in education. Schools have traditionally acknowledged the potential of drama and the arts in education by "wedging a few minutes of music and the visual arts into the school week and by occasionally putting on a play" (Shaw and Stevens 1979, xi). Usually viewed as enrichment activities, the arts are the first to be excluded from the educational program when budgets are cut or when national educational paranoia calls us back to basics. In particular, we seldom include drama in the educational experience as it could and should be included.

The educational activities and results of drama cannot pass the test of quantitative evaluation; and consequently drama is often considered soft in the face of economic restraint. Administrators then argue that moving drama and the arts aside can leave room for more practical schoolwork. Drama, however, can be a powerful educational tool as well as a fertile site for critical pedagogy.

It is my intention in this text to indicate some of the ways drama can be used as a site for critical pedagogy. There are, of course, many forms of drama being used in schools. These forms of drama cover a wide range from school plays to dramatic literature, from theatre arts to a method of learning. It is my intention to allow for these wide uses in any discussion on drama as a site for critical pedagogy. I plan to draw on the theory and practice of these varied forms as I search for a language of possibility. However, I do not mean this chapter to be an exhaustive reporting of drama. The literature on educational drama is very diffuse. The many and varied terms for "drama," along with myriad contextual placements, indicate the vastness of the subject within education. It is my hope to select from the various dramatic forms those aspects that promise to contribute to a critical pedagogy.

A systematic search of leading writers in educational drama presents the reader with an array of philosophies and suggested practices that can only confuse. Brian Way, a pioneer of drama education, claims that drama must concentrate on the whole person and that the emphasis must be on "developing people through drama" (1967, 2). Moses Golsberg offers a contrast to this claim for drama education when he writes that the prime function of pedagogy is to serve society "by molding children into citizens" (1974, 16).

An overview of the educational literature brings forth several drama terms that seem often to be used in interchangeable ways. These terms are: drama, theatre, educational drama, educational theatre, theatre arts, dramatic arts, creative arts, children's theatre, child drama, and drama in education. The literature further reveals that drama is found in a vast array of contrived arrangements with other subjects. The following represent some of the more common juxtapositions: speech and drama, speech and theatre, communications and drama, communications and theatre, language arts and drama, debate and drama, speech communication and drama, mythology and drama, theatre and dramatic arts, and, finally, poetry and theatre. This list, while not exhaustive, gives some sense of the ways drama is used in education.

The agitation generated in schools can be somewhat clarified by examining what is meant by "drama" and what is meant by "theatre." Gavin Bolton is most helpful in his discussions on the complex relationship between drama and theatre as they apply to schooling (Davis and Lawrence 1986). Bolton is correct in decrying the historical split that finds drama teachers in two opposite camps when it is clear, for pedagogical reasons, that drama and theatre need each other. Educators see drama as being primarily interested in human development and theatre as preoccupied with the acquisition of performance skills. Drama deals with process and theatre with product. Bolton argues, however, that teachers should think about drama and theatre being at opposite ends of a continuum rather than treated as separate categories. Teachers need to be able to move back and forth across that continuum to meet the particular educational needs of their students. There is considerable overlap between drama and theatre as it is found in schools. It has to be that way. Teachers and directors often use the same symbols, tensions, and skills to achieve differing ends. Critical drama pedagogy concerns itself with the crucial skills of interpreting, questioning, examining, focusing, reflecting, and sharing. Malcolm Ross (1982) realizes that drama, as used in education, must draw from theatre. It is important for educators to value the relationship between experiencing and presenting. This done in a reflective fashion, offers real hope for critical pedagogy.

In much of her writing, Maxine Greene (1978, 1980, 1990) points to new possibilities for drama within the educational process. Aesthetic experiences, she informs us, aid people in their pursuit of meaning and are part of the total lived experience of historical and social beings. The aesthetic realm cannot separate itself from the individual lives that experience it. Like Jean Paul

Sartre, Greene believes that a work of art demonstrates confidence in human freedom, which is the essence of transformation and emancipation.

Madeline Grumet (1980) postulates that drama in schools must do more than fill in the spaces of traditional formulas, must be willing to go beyond the predictable and point to possibility. Grumet would have teachers examine the symbols, rituals, and masks used in drama. These can be sharp tools for a critical drama pedagogy. With this form of drama, teachers and students can hope to be more aware of formal school rituals that celebrate authority, static roles, sentimentality, and the status quo. For example, the casting of school plays often replicates the social order of the classroom and the greater community. Who gets the good parts? Who gets to select the play to be rehearsed and presented? Do teachers choose plays that speak to or about the lives of students? The plays presented rarely reflect the tensions or conflicts that exist between teacher, students, and community. In this way because the tension and conflict on stage may have no real connection with the audience, cast, or crew, the exercise is safe. The play usually has a happy ending, the audience goes away smiling, and the distance between play and reality is maintained. The play divorces itself from the intention and culture that generated it. There are times when drama, even school drama, should create dissonance and make the audience uncomfortable. We could replace passive acceptance with resistance to the negative aspects of the status quo. A cry of resistance is a sign of hope. If there was no hope, resistance would be futile, but since there is hope, resistance is necessary. Drama in schools must work to provoke a critical response from its audience and a reflective commitment from its directors and actors. The world of the student must come face to face with the reality of the audience. Here we can see how drama and theatre, as they are traditionally separated, could complement each other. Drama taps the student resources that could be the basis for a script, and theatre presents the developed play. By building on student resources, teachers can also reinterpret scripted plays. I will address this concept more fully in chapter five, where

I look at a cross section of popular published plays. I will examine these plays in view of their potential for critical pedagogy.

David Hornbrook (1989) claims that school drama should "help students understand their dramatic culture" (p. 13). This means that teachers who use drama in their work must be aware of their own dramatic culture. It is the teacher who must be able to cross back and forth between reality and fiction, as well as between reproduced and produced culture. To do this it is necessary to be critically aware of the traditional philosophies and pedagogical uses of drama. A presentation of alternative models will help give a wider scope to, and demonstrate the possibilities of, drama education.

HISTORY OF DRAMA

The essence of drama is our interaction with the total environment and a struggle to understand the significance of lived experience. Coming to grips with this lived experience has to be a primary task of education. I have indicated earlier that drama education has been used in varied forms to help with this task. The most accessible form of literature for the young and the yet-to-be-educated, drama is basic for it puts us at the level of sensation and calls on the whole person to respond. The intellect can further engage the dramatic. Drama follows life and as such comments on it. Drama is beyond literature for it is mime and talk and script. Drama is alive; that is, it is in motion and in relief. Dennis Mulcahy (1991) claims that drama must be treated as dynamic in the sense that it changes and evolves over time. Drama is prior to literature in so far as it deals with the life of experience on which literature rests. Drama is the source from which other literary forms and discourses flow.

The use of drama in education is not new. Gavin Bolton's (1984) fine history of drama in education attests to this. Drama has been long recognized as a pedagogical tool used both for education and indoctrination. Critical pedagogy concerns itself with the margin between education and indoctrination. In many ways, we force ourselves to go back to our fundamental reasons for education because we need to have our own philosophies of education worked out before attempting to use drama. As I previously mentioned, teaching drama is a lot like walking an educational tightrope. Teachers and students are not dealing with neat formulas or mathematical equations in drama. That there is real opportunity to roam educationally is both the strength and danger of using drama in the process of schooling. Teachers of drama have possibly more control over content, resources, and methodology. This control is a great opening for teachers as well as a burden for them. Drama teachers, and teachers who use drama, have an opportunity to formulate their own curriculum. This is a major break for teachers who wish to see themselves as transformative intellectuals (Aronowitz and Giroux 1985). Teachers can never see themselves in such a way as long as curriculum is developed at some other site. Curriculum needs to be seen as the events, activities, and interactions that are experienced in the classroom setting. Drama teachers can have tremendous control over their own professional work.

Drama education can differ from that of the past. Our present use of drama has evolved naturally in the mainstream of modern educational thought. Drama's origins go back to Plato, Aristotle, Rabelais, and Rousseau. Drama is informed by social anthropology, child psychology, and the developmental psychology of Piaget.

Plato and Aristotle based their concepts of education on play. However, Plato's idealism would banish theatre from his Republic. Aristotle, on the other hand, demonstrated that people learned through imitation and that the theatre could purge the person of impure emotions. Even though the Roman philosophers followed Aristotle's view on the importance of imitation, the early medieval Church was opposed to most forms of secular dramatic activity. By the Renaissance, drama was again seen as an inherent part of education.

Dramatic education suffered a setback in the eighteenth century. In time the Romantic philosophers again expressed the virtues of play and imitation. Goethe encouraged the use of both improvisation and performance in education while Rousseau claimed that play and work should be synonymous. During the present century a philosophy of drama has evolved and now seems to be part of educational thought. This grounding philosophy starts with the child as child and recognizes that dramatic imagination is an essential human quality.

We can observe the full range of dramatic play in every civilized society with each society developing its own specific characteristics. A developed culture, in great part, bases itself upon play; drama and ritual are the sophisticated versions of many of the mechanisms inherent in child play. It would seem that both the play of the child and the theatre of the adult represent human attempts to find expression and security.

Richard Courtney (1974) advices us that drama is an important method of communication within a society and that the cultural pattern and the dramatic enactment interrelate. As drama and theatre developed, stable civilizations gave rise to religious enactments, and ritual eventually became liturgy. In time theatre emerged from the temple and the bond between ritual and liturgy was loosened to allow drama to become more secular. Each society developed its own dramatic patterns. These patterns are expressed in folk plays, ballads, fairs, circuses, carnivals, and became part of our dramatic inheritance.

Nellie McCaslin (1980) claims that the twentieth century was well advanced before the arts began to have any real impact on public education. Drama followed music, athletics, and the visual arts into the curriculum. Helen Jagerman (1987) reminds us that the lack of formal education among drama teachers and the elective status of high school arts courses gives drama education a reduced position in the curriculum. Possibly one of the greatest banes of a drama teacher's life is to be asked to put on a play for some school occasion. This request often reflects the value given to drama in schools. Most drama teachers want their own and their students' work to be more than an ornament or event. Few people today would argue against the value of drama in schooling, yet it sits in an uneasy place.

PEDAGOGICAL USES

In this section I want to examine the pedagogical uses of drama. These pedagogical uses will further indicate existing practices in drama. The models presented here are given to represent what leading teachers and writers perceive drama education to be. In referring to pedagogical uses, I am including all the possible ways drama can be used in a school setting. This range could cover the use of drama from helping students understand a given event in any aspect of the wider curriculum to presenting a fully scripted play before an audience. There are many arenas for using drama between these two extremes.

There is a sense in which all effective teaching in the classroom is dramatic by its very nature. The relationship within the classroom is dynamic, for there is constant interplay between the teacher and students. The teacher should not disallow the role of actor and misinterpret it as a negative statement about instruction. Of course teachers are actors in the best sense of the term. Teaching is a group situation with strong dramatic overtones; learning is not just a process if imparting and receiving instruction. The best teaching and learning occur when the teacher-actor is drawing out the student-actors in much the same way a director teases out a role from a stage actor. One of the reasons drama is so valuable an activity educationally is that it allows the teacher to capitalize on the inherent dramatic characteristics of the classroom. Drama is a natural for education.

Drama can be an improvisational, noninhibiting process based on human impulse and ability to act out perceptions of the world to understand it. In such drama, the teacher guides participants to imagine and reflect upon the human experience. The group improvises action and dialogue as they explore, develop, express, and communicate ideas, concepts, and feelings through dramatic enactment. This exercise is quite different from the traditional putting on a play. Elements of theatre provide focus and structure, but in the school setting the goal is often beyond the entertainment of an audience. As far as some educators are concerned, the growth of the individual is the goal of drama. Brian Way (1967) claims that the development of the whole person must be the goal of concentration. Way opposes drama seen as another subject, simply adding to the intensification of teacher work. Way's work did much to make a distinction between drama and theatre by driving a wedge between experiencing and presenting. However, because we often see only performance as the final goal of a drama curriculum, we could lose sight of the many values in the broader educational use of drama. In the view of Richard Courtney (1984) drama is more than play and more than entertainment. Drama can be a vital part of school life and contribute to the overall education of an individual student.

Educators claim that long-term involvement in a drama process develops the whole person physically, intellectually, and emotionally. According to such educators, drama stimulates logical and intuitive thinking, personalizes knowledge, and yields aesthetic pleasure. The process helps the total student and teacher by promoting positive self-concepts, social awareness, and empathy. Drama can further aid in the clarification of attitudes and in the articulation of moral standards of behavior. In a true sense, a drama curriculum can go beyond itself to be a vital means of developing skills, knowledge, and sensitivity that would seem to be basic to a complete education. This is not to argue that drama time is magic time; as I said earlier, drama is a tool. As such, it depends very much on its use.

> Drama can be used as a learning medium throughout the school age years. By mid-adolescence most people have created a "symbolic net," part shared symbols, part their own symbols. To take the students to even higher forms of consciousness, educators should be exposing students to the magnificent weave of discursive and non-discursive symbols found in drama. (Juliebo, Thiessen, and Bain 1991, 8)

The diversity of drama activities provides opportunities for the involvement of all students regardless of experience, cultural background, or disadvantaged conditions. This concept can be rather surprising if drama is not seen in its widest sense. Drama is inherently exciting and stimulating. Drama is more than just a class or school play, more than an extracurricular activity, and much more than a medium of entertainment. It is a vital and viable teaching technique. "If you want to know what a child is, study his play, if you want to affect what he shall be, direct the form of his play" (McSweeney 1974, 9). The ways of directing this play are wide and varied. So much depends on how the given educator sees the aim of drama education.

Dramatic activities can involve choice at several different levels. By assuming a role, taking a stance, or setting up a character, the student is trying out a version of self without making a permanent commitment. In so doing the student is both choosing and laying a basis for future choices. Students do this in the safety of drama, that fictional place they can make their own. Students can act out their fears and desires in symbolic form and in so doing can better assimilate these into their lives. Moreover, the element of role-playing, or the putting on of a mask, allows the student to handle situations that could be dangerous in a class setting other than drama. This fact has application for living as well as schooling. For those students who are deprived of a wide range of social experiences, dramatic recreation of real life situations may be an important way of developing control over a range of registers. For many students, drama could be an important creative medium, since it demands less verbal explicitness and is inseparable from expressive movement. In short, drama does not limit itself to one form of expression or exploration. One of the great attractions drama holds for me is that it can be realized on so many levels. Drama can be truly multidimensional because it employs dialogue, sound, symbol, and movement. Drama also makes use of silence, vacancy, and stillness. It is often in silence, vacancy, and stillness that drama speaks loudest. These offer interesting openings for a critical pedagogy.

Drama can engage students, lure their interest, entice them to participate, captivate their imaginations, and push them into exciting new worlds. We are most excited when we go that one step beyond where we were, when we go beyond ourselves. Drama allows students, as well as teachers, to go to that new world almost without knowing it. In a sense a student can hide behind drama, which can serve as an emotional cover for that student. Drama can be a place to risk failure from behind a mask or from within a role. If there is success within the drama, then students can carry this new-found gift back to real life and use it in other ways. Patrick Verriour (1989) talks about the drama of drama.

> Drama has the power to place children in a position [*sic*] to take risks in their learning without fear of penalty, to face and deal with human issues and problems . . . as well as to reflect on the implications of choices and decisions they have made in the dramatic context. (285)

Leading writers and teachers use drama in various ways giving rise to questions concerning the use of such drama. As might be expected from what I have said already, teachers use drama in many ways in schools. Drama may be used for a particular purpose or in a fashion that reflects the educational perspective of a certain teacher.

Cecily O'Neill in *Drama Guidelines* (1976) expresses the long-term aim of drama teaching as helping students to understand themselves. With this aim the drama teacher is trying to set up situations within which students can discover why people behave as they do. The active involvement with a fictitious situation is the strength of drama education. This fictitious involvement offers great opportunities for critical pedagogy. A secondary aim is for students to achieve understanding of and satisfaction from the medium of drama. Drama, like all the arts in education, has its own intrinsic value.

Much is claimed about drama. Educators claim that drama can teach the basic organizational skills of categorizing, classifying, and sequencing. It can teach perceptual skills to organize sensory messages and to give meaning to them.

Drama can teach auditory perception: rhythm, timing, hearing likeness and differences, remembering sounds and words, and remembering them in the proper order. We usually think of these skills as being needed for drama and hardly ever as drama giving such skills.

Drama can teach visual perception: seeing likenesses and differences, remembering what has been seen, and remembering several things in order. All this happens under the guise of doing drama. Drama can teach motor skills: movement using the whole body, parts of the body, eye-hand coordination, eye-foot coordination, rhythm, and timing. Planning how to use the body effectively within a given space can also be a part of drama.

Drama can teach language skills by introducing new vocabulary systematically, by offering opportunities for verbal expressions, modeling phrases for students to repeat, by playing with word sounds. It follows that drama helps with verbal confidence.

On another level, drama can teach symbolism: this gesture, that facial expression, this movement, and that sound can stand for something. Drama can teach to isolate a main characteristic to convey meaning.

William Akins (1981) writes that at the outset, drama in education was employed as a teaching tool, a means of providing cultural enrichment, a medium for social interaction, and as a form of supervised recreation. Educators see drama as encouraging creative expression. It is Akins' view that, along with opportunities for the exercise of judgment, drama can involve students in the culture of a society. In particular, the students culture is crucial in critical pedagogy.

Literature helps the reader to experience events, situations, and emotions vicariously; drama helps a student get inside the consciousness of other human beings and to experience a critical segment of life. In this way, educational drama takes students beyond reading and plunges them into the activity of an assumed person. With such activity the students can compose the role as they go along, and often in a direct fashion, are able to transcend and possibly transform their own circumstances. Henrik Ibsen's comment in 1874 may still be apt for the use of educational drama: "A student has essentially the same task as the poet: to make clear to himself, and thereby to others, the temporal and eternal questions that are astir in the community to which he belongs" (Shuman 1978, 158). In this sense, drama is basic to understanding what it means to be human and how society operates. This is the raw material of a critical drama pedagogy.

The work of Dorothy Heathcote has done much to advance the cause of educational drama. Heathcote defines educational drama as being anything that involves persons in active role-taking situations in which attitudes and not characters are the chief concern (Wagner 1979; Hornbrook 1989). Heathcote sees drama more as a system than as a subject. Way (1967) agrees in part when he writes that drama should not be simply another subject fitted into an already overcrowded curriculum. However, Way does not agree that drama should be seen only as a useful tool for teaching other subjects. He wrote that drama has first to exist within its own right. When the aspects of drama are experienced and mastered, then it may be a helpful tool for other areas in education. The role that the teacher plays in drama education is imperative. Teachers, according to Way, have to remind themselves that what they are concerned with is the development of every one of the many facets of being human. At the beginning of drama the teacher is concerned with helping students to discover and explore their own resources. In a stage that might come later, drama would include the discovery and exploration of the students' environment. With this approach to drama education, the teacher would help the students work at their own rate to seek various levels of selected personal attributes.

In a contrasting view, John Allen (1979) claims that drama is indeed a subject and as such is probably the newest on the curriculum, having reached some kind of respectability during the 1960s. This view of drama as a subject is supported by other educational writers and practiced by many teachers in various school settings. Many high schools now have discrete subjects classified as drama or theatre arts. Again the educational practice is wide and varied.

Writers in the field approach drama education from different view points. A further review of the literature on drama education reveals differences in underlying assumptions held by writers in the field. We now know that such underlying assumptions are far from neutral and that they direct the very outcomes of education (McCaslin 1980; Hornbrook 1989).

THE RELATIONSHIP OF DRAMA AND THEATRE

Drama education takes many expressed forms. Given the many aims behind drama's use, it could hardly be otherwise. The various terms employed and noted earlier in this chapter lead to confusion for students and teachers of drama. There is a further lack of consistency from writers within the field. It might be helpful in this section to examine the more salient terms used within the area of drama education.

One of the terms we often read about is creative drama. On one hand, creative drama may make use of a story with a beginning, a middle, and an end. On the other hand, it may explore, develop, and express ideas and feelings through dramatic enactment. Students can create dialogue with content taken from a well known story or they can work from an original idea. In creative drama, the dialogue lines are not necessarily written down or memorized. In this process the drama builds on itself so that it becomes more detailed and better organized as it grows. Creative drama remains extemporaneous, and the entertainment of an audience is seldom part of the design. The aim of the process is the optimal growth and development of the students.

The Children's Theatre Association of America has accepted the following definition of creative drama.

> Creative drama is improvisational, non-exhibitional, process-centered form of drama in which participants are guided by a leader to imagine, enact, and reflect upon human experiences. Although creative drama traditionally has been thought of in

relation to children and young people, the process is appropriate to all ages. (McCaslin 1980, 8)

Children's theatre refers to the formal productions for children's audiences. The actors in such productions can be either amateurs or professionals, children or adults, or any combination. Such plays are directed and dialogue is memorized with costumes and scenery often playing an important part. Unlike creative drama, children's theatre is audience-centered. The goal is to provide the best theatrical experience for the audience. These two references give us the polarities represented by the terms drama and theatre.

It is easy to see how there can be an educational split between creative drama and children's theatre. One has to do with develop-ment and the other has to do with performance. This split has widened over the last two decades. The claim has been that the distinction between drama and theatre is necessary in so far as both call for different aims and pedagogical uses. Hornbrook claims that the distinctions made so forcefully by some teachers between their drama and that going on in the theatre, remain less than compre-hensible. The various terms quoted in the beginning of this chapter reflect the contrived usage of either drama or theatre, and as such should indicate an emphasis either on personal development or performance for an audience. It is my contention that this exagger-ated split is overplayed and nonproductive. Firman Brown (1991) claims that somewhere along the way "performance-production people" and the "theatre-education people" moved away from each other and lost the commonalty that they shared in the art form. We are victims of that separation. Both sides of the choosing are less because of that enforced schism. Martin Esslin's (1978) claim that theatre is stage drama is helpful in its simplicity. In this sense, theatre is the controlled expression of drama. This might be a place for us to start.

Some leaders in the field have warned against the use of drama to achieve other ends. This warning shows a genuine concern on the part of drama teachers and would seem to indicate the need for a coherent theory of aesthetic education. This concern is not to be confused with the integration of drama with other subjects. Nellie McCaslin (1980) points out that projects integrating drama, music, dance, creative writing, and the visual arts with literature and social studies have been popular for some time. In this way drama becomes a basic part of the educational system rather than existing on the fringe. This type of subject integration calls for staff and administrative cooperation.

Teachers dictate how drama is used in the classroom depending on their philosophical and educational aims. Consequently it seems so important for educators to rethink the general objectives of drama in schools. Gavin Bolton (1984) states that focus, tension, and symbolization, the very tools that the playwright and director use, are also the tools of educational drama. It is, I believe, virtually impossible to be involved in educational drama without using these tools. Educational dramatists must acknowledge the legacy of theatre.

Dorothy Heathcote gives us some hint of how to see the value of more closely linking drama and theatre. Edwards and Craig (1990) refer to Heathcote's classifications of the elements of theatre used in classroom drama as darkness and light, silence and sound, as well as stillness and movement. It is not a long stretch to realize that these elements of theatre are the working parts of school drama. Heathcote works "from the inside out" and attempts to expand students' understanding of life experiences. She would have her students reflect on a particular circumstance and seek to make sense out of their world in a deeper way. Heathcote, who thinks that drama should be used in all areas of curriculum begins with process and in time moves to presentation that may take an audience into account. However, performance is not her major concern. Her intent is to give depth and breadth to learning. Heathcote seeks out the dramatic juncture in an event or a unit of study. In this particular use of drama, teachers need to be able to discover the tension and conflict of a given setting and use its educative moment. Heathcote sees value in isolating an event through dramatization so that the teacher can negotiate with students while building on their ideas and experiences. Brad Haseman

(1991) reinforces this point when he claims that drama must be a collaboration between the teacher and the students. He insists that an agreement to do drama with students is negotiated.

Many educators welcome the Heathcote approach of meeting objectives not met by other methods or resources. Brian Way (1967) in his early writings was not interested in training actors but in developing people. Way does not see the arts as another academic subject concerned with the development of intellect. Way concerns himself with the development of intuition, which he feels needs training as does the intellect. This intangible and immeasurable factor makes it difficult for the academic mind to accept intuition as part of general education.

Way would have teachers in drama education start from the point where they are most interested and confident. He expressed a fear of detailed and systematic programs where the teacher and students follow rigid lockstep procedures. The drama teacher should not impose a whole new set of possibly artificial factors but start with those facets of human beings that are found in all people. What the student experiences and demonstrates in the classroom is most important. In the early stages Way sees the teacher's task as helping with the what and not the how of a particular dramatic experience. The end product is not the focus of concentration, which would be the case in a strictly theatre program. As indicated, Way is quite conscious of the distinction between drama and theatre.

In her book *A Space Where Anything Can Happen* Rosilyn Wilder (1977) claims that drama is not just a set of techniques and methods. She sees drama as an approach or a way to connect with something special within each student. Wilder claims students can do this by dramatizing anything within potential human experience. Drama, she would claim, allows students to internalize learning through a unified physical, mental, and emotional experience. Students can then integrate this experience into greater human understanding.

Wilder does not see drama as a series of activities pulled out now and then as rainy day projects, and she does not recommend creative manuals and activity packets. Wilder puts great emphasis on the value of creative learning that depends on the attitude and approach of the teacher. In this use of drama, the teacher is a careful listener, stimulator, and facilitator who teases out and builds upon a student's values, ideas, and abilities.

Cecily O'Neill (1976) expresses another point on the drama and theatre continuum when she indicates that there has been a shift from an interest in the personal development of the individual pupil to the recognition of drama as a precise teaching instrument. This particular method works best, according to O'Neill, when drama is seen as part of the learning process and when it is firmly embedded within the school curriculum. In this view drama is no longer seen only as another branch of arts education but as a unique teaching tool, which is vital in language development and invaluable in the exploration of other subject areas.

As indicated above, Bolton maintains that the same "clay" is being used by drama theatre people. It might well be time for educators on both sides of the debate to realize the value of thinking and working together (not necessarily the same, just together). Drama students can both learn and perform. For many years, many of us, working in drama education, saw no need to make such distinctions between drama and theatre. This distinction, somewhat analogous to traders bringing tobacco back to Europe, we could well do without. In relation to the on-going struggle between drama and theatre, David Hornbrook (1990) states "We must bury forever that historical but damaging distinction between drama and theatre. Conceptually there is nothing which differentiates the child acting in the classroom from the actor on the stage of the theatre" (p. 7).

As Tony Jackson (1980) commented some time earlier, education can take place in many ways. "Any good theatre will itself be educational—i.e., when it initiates or extends a questioning process in its audience, when it makes us look again, freshly, at the world, its institutions and conventions and at our place in that world." (p. 22).

In the given sampling of the use of drama in education, I have referred to examples that have personal development as the major aim with performance for an audience only as a secondary or occasional consequence. However, the use of theatre in schools, with its performance orientation, is well documented and seems to be a dominant model. It is time, I think, to strike a balance between development and performance and explore ways that give students the best of both worlds.

EXPERIENCING AND PRESENTING

In this section on experiencing and presenting in drama, I hope to indicate the emancipatory possibilities for that process in schooling. One place to start would be with some of the alternative forms of drama education. These alternative forms indicate to me that there can indeed be a drama pedagogy that is grounded within a critical perspective. Certainly drama has tremendous critical possibilities for schooling.

For educational drama to function in the classroom, certain conditions are necessary. Students and teachers in a school setting must have relationships that allow them to be confident enough to take on dramatic roles. They should feel that they are valued as people and that each person has a contribution to make. The teacher's role is crucial at this juncture.

The rise of the New Sociology of Education brought with it a debate imperative to fundamental issues in education. Those of us who saw the aesthetic as having a key place in a transformed schooling process did not miss this point. The goals of people like Michael Young and Basil Bernstein were to liberate teacher and student from social, institutional, and intellectual constraints by a critical examination of the taken-for-granted assumptions that surround schooling. Part of this ongoing struggle is to convince ourselves, as teachers, that we must continue to learn. There must be a dialectical relationship between teaching and learning. Teaching is not a position where you ever arrive. The first contested ground for transformation must always be the teacher's own knowledge. There is transformation, or at least freedom, in accepting the dialectical nature of teaching and learning. Schools must be places where both teacher and student grow (Doyle 1989).

Writers like Maxine Greene (1990), Roger Simon (1987), and Madeline Grumet (1980) have built on the ideas from the New Sociology of Education and are bringing a critical perspective to aesthetics and drama in particular. Within the philosophic framework for reconceptualization, there needs to be a concern for the intrinsic nature and quality of educational experience, which is apart from the utilitarian function for the achievement of goals. Concerning the value of drama in education this idea is important. Some philosophies of drama education are heavily utilitarian. Greene continues to point the way to alternate modes of curriculum inquiry. Turning her emphasis more toward the value of the aesthetic in education, Greene avoids seeing drama as a tool and tends to place much more emphasis on the personal meaning in any curriculum, drama education included.

> So many of us today confine ourselves to right angles. We function in the narrowest of specialities; we lead one-dimensional lives. We accommodate ourselves so easily to the demands of the technological society—to time schedules, charts, programs, techniques—that we lose touch with our streams of consciousness, our inner time. (Greene 1978, 199)

This philosophy is important for any possible emancipatory drama pedagogy because the tools of technology, modern administration, and the rationality of dominance hold sway over culture. Such notions hold sway over culture in ways we cannot always see or seldom find help to realize in the process of schooling. Drama education, if it is to be critical education, must not come down on the side of the utilitarian. Greene speaks strongly to the emancipatory possibilities of using aesthetics in education for she writes of the "pursuit of meaning" and not the utilitarian use of a subject like drama. Greene claims that aesthetic experiences involve existing beings who are in pursuit of meaning. In short that implies being social and being historical. According to Greene we work out our own reality in a world that we have constituted for ourselves.

Much of this educational examination, following on the early work of Young and others, allows us to slip the surly bonds of institutional and intellectual constraints. Drama can help this process. Simon (1987) gives positive modes of the use of drama as a transformative process. Simon concerns himself with an inquiry into the development and maintenance of social settings. The second aspect of this inquiry is to help understand the dynamics of social life in a way that will allow reflective dialogue, which in turn will allow the development of future action.

Grumet's distinction between ritual and theatre, as both apply to schooling, is informative to an understanding of a critical pedagogy of drama: "Theatre as a deliberate aesthetic enterprise, is the only mode of theatre that contains form and confrontation and thus may contribute to the transformation of the culture of the school" (1980, 96).

Drama, can, I believe, be a vehicle of recognition and indictment. This removes drama and drama's use in schooling far from the pleasure principle of the comfortable and gives it back its critical and transformative teeth. Drama should be free not only to reflect on life but to point to life's possibilities.

Much of the work directly related to drama education done by reconceptualist thinkers is done by way of critique. By this I mean the work has been done to warn us of the traps in the educative processes. This is valid; yet, I believe that a positive critical theory of drama education is needed.

As I have claimed a number of times in these chapters, drama in its widest educational use remains flagrantly acritical. As such drama refuses to articulate an interest in individual and social transformative action. Drama refuses the challenge to treat dialectically the relationships between the individual and society. It is possible that models of drama pedagogy can concentrate on aims that treat the subject as object and in isolation. The drama student, then, seems not to be regarded as a subject within a culture that is in formation. I have grounded this text in the belief that things can change, and new possibilities within the lived experience can be envisioned and realized. Drama education, not content with working solely on student development and reproducing entertaining plays, can take a critical interest in individual and social transformative action and can help teachers see their role in a more critical perspective.

4

Drama and Critical Pedagogy

Player: Audiences know what to expect, and that is all they are
prepared to believe in.
      Tom Stoppard, *Rosencrantz and Guildenstern Are Dead*

Driving these chapters is a nagging question about how teachers
can help students obtain the skills to examine the imposed assumptions behind their aesthetic and social worlds. In this particular
chapter I will indicate the work of some aesthetics educators who
use various forms of drama in a fashion that allows for a critical
pedagogy. I will use drama in this context not only as a social act
but as an indicator and creator of critical consciousness.

Where does drama fit into the larger scheme of critical pedagogy? Having attempted to understand the role and influence of
schools, critical pedagogy wishes to empower people and transform society. Drama contributes to this process by probing questions and offering suggestions that can be dramatically open or
provided through metaphor. Those of us who work with drama
must realize that the scripts we present to our students and colleagues are not neutral, value-free, asocial, or ahistorical. Since
these scripts represent a snatch of someone's life and circum-

stances, we can examine them for the light they allow on someone else's reality and, therefore, on our own.

I believe that aesthetic experience, and in particular drama education, holds within itself a language of possibility. It is necessary to probe deeply into the educational theory and practice of drama to find examples of critical moments, but such moments can be found and illuminated. It is also necessary to examine the oppositional and emancipatory elements (Giroux 1984) that exist in drama in developing a site for critical pedagogy.

For purposes of clarity I wish to note here that I am examining educators who work with drama across the continuum. This perspective is necessary because, in the total picture of schooling drama is practiced across such a broad range. I admit I come down on the side of process rather than product. The inherent dialectic of drama in its various forms will need to be explored for its critical possibilities.

In chapter one I commented on the contributions of critical theory to drama. Having presented the relationships of drama to critical ideas of society, culture, and aesthetics, I believe elements of this presentation can form the basis for a theory of critical drama pedagogy. There will be an attempt to apply these elements from critical theory to existing models of drama with a view to expanding their critical moments. I pointed out at the close of the last chapter that there is great ambiguity in the field of drama as it is used in education. On the surface the majority of education models are united in their resistance to critical pedagogy. Drama seems to offer fertile ground for a critical examination of a variety of entrenched educational thinking. This situation comes in part from the pliable nature of drama, which in turn offers a viable reflection for all things great and small. However, few of these drama models articulate an interest in individual and social transformation or emancipation. Generally these models do not treat dialectically the relationship between the individual and society or point to the promise of emancipatory critique and action.

The essence of drama is human interaction with the social environment and the struggle to understand the significance of the lived experience. As Dorothy Heathcote claims drama is a real person in a mess. I stated earlier that critical theory seeks to understand all social practices that hinder self-consciousness and free development. Drama, if it is to be part of a critical education, needs to ask how it currently fits social practices that hinder self-consciousness or free development.

Education must do more than serve society by molding children into predetermined citizens. To serve society better in realizing its potential, drama might show that the values, attitudes, and actions of that society cannot be seen as perennial but are subject to positive change. Such a view of drama can allow for the cultural capital that varied children may bring to the schooling process. Notions like fitting into existing society (Golsberg 1974) help us understand why the powerless accept their fate. Critical drama, on the other hand, does not have a place for such a notion for notions such as these allow drama within educational institutions to make official a culture that can well be the property of dominant groups. By dominant, in this context, I mean the people and institutions who have the social power to dictate, often by apparent consent, what culture is to be. This is a crucial concept in the development of any critical pedagogy. Cultural domination can be more subtle than political or economic domination, or the imposition of brute force, but the domination is no less destructive.

REFINING THE VALUE OF DRAMA

Drama, dealing as it does with tension and conflict, is able to develop a critical discourse, that is, a discourse that invites opposition and argument. In this way drama resists the temptation to resolve contradictions in a spurious harmony. By allowing argument and discourse, drama, in its own form and in its own structure, can show the contradictions of social reality. Cecily O'Neill (1991) is correct in pointing out that the language of transformation is found in the vocabulary of theatre. "Theatre metaphors illuminate an idea of teaching that is essentially dialogic, and therefore dynamic, democratic, social, demystifying, and open to transformation" (p. 23). The drama teacher must operate inside the process by affirming the skills learned from their own theatre and using them in their drama teaching. The idea is for one to build on the other because the power of theatre gets lived out on the classroom floor.

Earlier I claimed that culture is the expression of human consciousness shaped by social living. Richard Courtney (1984) says that the expression of culture comes in dramatic forms. It is important to realize that each society develops its own dramatic patterns, which form part of our cultural inheritance. However, we have to ask how drama is used to objectify a given culture either through conscious intention or simply as a result of entrenched attitudes. Remembering Antonio Gramsci's hegemony, as well as Pierre Bourdieu's symbolic violence will help us guard against allowing drama to be used to devalue and invalidate certain cultures. We cannot abandon our schools to the demands of any one cultural group. We have to realize that teaching drama is a cultural activity; Reynolds and Skilbeck (1976) call drama a cultural project.

> Two kinds of curriculum and teaching strategies may be distinguished: those which equip students with the means to interpret, assess, and redefine what they are taught, and those which promote acquiescence and passive acceptance. It is within the power and should be part of the responsibility of the teacher to encourage pupils to be more reflective, critical, and analytic. (p. 85)

Catherine Belsey (1980) expresses this critical quest when she refers to Bertolt Brecht's invitation to his audience to become actively engaged in criticizing his plays. Brecht wanted the audience to be more than consumers of his art, to go beyond admiration for his genius, and to really see the play.

Courtney (1984) tells us that the cultural patterns of the audience materially alter playwriting and acting and that there is a close interdependence between the playhouse, the audience, and the performance. Students need to be involved in the process of making drama. Teachers should allow students to think like playwrights, performers, designers, and directors. Life in the theatre is so departmentalized: writers write, directors direct, designers design, and performers perform. While it is impossible to reproduce or produce a play without the work of its various contributors we often operate as if all these acts are separate. Even though schools should not take their lead from professional theatre, the process of theatre needs to be brought into the classroom. This process calls for intellectual, physical, and emotive activity (Wright 1991). We notice this fact in a positive way when we see a large number of high-school students and teachers writing and presenting their own plays. These plays usually grow out of the shared life of a community and are performed for the community and in this way become part of the produced culture of that community. This communal value alone speaks to the critical possibilities of drama because here we are not talking only about performance but about a process that is essential to cultural production. Drama in this instance is not simply a reflection of culture but a critical interaction with that culture. Consider, for example, the potential effects of a mirror on self-image. If I look into a mirror I make an image and the reflected image can cause me to make changes to my expression or my clothing. Similarly, a presented drama not only reflects the culture from which it grew but can help that culture change. It follows that drama helps to produce or reproduce culture. We miss much of the potential for drama if we do not realize that it can play a part in reformulating culture just as it does in objectifying it. Drama is always produced and interpreted within given social conditions, yet it is not simply determined by such conditions. We have what Rex Gibson calls "complex reciprocity" (1986, 97). Drama, like other forms of art, must face up to the real world around it. There is an interdependence between culture, economics, and drama. Drama teachers should look to the world of the students and not limit themselves to plot, character, and form, which are important aspects of drama but are not necessarily transformative.

One of the difficulties with art in schools is that it tends to be what the teacher makes it so that the teacher's background, interests and attitudes often become the focus for the drama program. This is fine when we talk about teacher autonomy in developing curriculum, but there can be cultural sand-traps. Undoubtedly the cultural capital of the teacher will be a dominant factor in shaping a drama program in school, yet teachers need to be aware of the cultural capital of the students. If it is to serve the best interests of the students, the drama program should reflect and build on their cultural capital. Teachers need to be honest and reflective enough to stand back from their own teaching and ask whose culture is being indicated, affirmed, and transmitted. It is at this juncture that teachers can realize a critical moment for drama education and act upon that moment. Teachers can give a voice to students who normally would speak neither for themselves nor their families. It is here that a teacher can, through in-role work, help students realize the authentic value of different lifestyles, ethnic origins, or belief systems. Writers of drama often claim that drama can help students assume responsibility, accept decisions, and work together cooperatively (McCaslin 1980). If this is so, then a critical drama should ask questions concerning that responsibility, those decisions, and cooperative work. Whose interests are being served? What responsibility is being nurtured and toward whom? In what work and to what ends are students to cooperate? Drama can aid in the achievement of many aims, but teachers and students should know what these aims are as well as the reasoning behind them. In this way, teachers develop some control over their work and students gain some faith in their education.

One of the pitfalls of teaching is the tendency to help students fulfill only the ambitions teachers have for them. Many of us working in education have long realized that the most successful students are the ones most like their teachers. Brian Way (1967) has promoted the growth and acceptance of drama education with his emphasis on personal development and the development of intuition in individuals. Way's positive attitudes concerning personal development can, I believe, be expanded to include drama's role in consciousness formation. We need to go beyond Way's work and help students be critical of the society they inherit. Drama as a tool of criticism allows students to see the promise in a given society and can help form the consciousness of human agents who can then aid in the transformation of that society. Drama teachers have to move beyond the notion that the full development of the individual, constrained by the tenets of a given society, is sufficient. The development of the individual, even complete with intuition and uniqueness, is not enough, for the given reality is not enough, not sufficient. Drama, to be a critical form of pedagogy, must come down on the side of transformative critique and action. Only in this way can students be free and help society change for the better.

DRAMA EDUCATORS

Drama, in its various forms, is a primary source of information for the late-twentieth-century North American. Charlotte Motter (1970) claims that if schools are to prepare students to live in North American society, schools must offer these students the opportunity to acquire a basic education in the theatre arts. What would Motter have her students acquire? Would she allow her students to criticize the society they get to know through theatre arts? Would she have her students realize the impact that movies, television, and the other products of the cultural industry have on the way they see, accept, and appreciate social reality? If not, drama education could fall right into the manipulative hands of the culture industry. This cultural industry calls for the consumer, the patron, the playgoer to be acritical and merely echo the standards of the status quo. Drama treated in this fashion can be used by the culture industry to replace consciousness with conformity. If used in this way, drama will impede the development of autonomous, independent, and critical individuals.

It seems that in Motter's work the products of the culture are taken to represent given and eternal truths. She writes as if drama education in high school is primarily general education in the arts and humanities, and that it is designed to enhance the cultural and aesthetic background of the students and that what is offered to the students is the best of the culture and society. However, there needs to be an agenda that sees dialectically the conditions of lived experience and an opening for a critical perspective on the relationships between the individual and society. Motter claims that producing a play helps the student learn the importance of cooperating with a large group of individuals, each of whom has an assignment that is integral to the whole production. There is danger here of collapsing the concepts of part and whole. Concerning these Motter writes: "Drama activity emphasizes the interrelation of the parts and the indispensability of each to the whole, and illustrates the importance of obeying the established chain of command vital to any successful cooperative endeavor" (p. 5). While this may be a very pragmatic posture for producing a play, it certainly does not speak to a critical or an emancipatory approach to drama.

One of the critical needs of drama is the very opposite of this. A critical drama pedagogy should have the capacity to transcend the doubtful unity of subject and object, part and whole. Telling students that they are part of the whole may be fostering a notion that does lead away from emancipatory thought or action.

One of the main tools of the culture industry is its use of style. Motter reinforces this trend when she writes that "the student learns the techniques of establishing a mood that will evoke the desired emotional response from the audience" by light, color, and sound (p. 6). Critical theorists tell us that style captivates, but in the face of it, we often remain acritical. In this way drama can be a means of administering culture. The message can be subsumed in the style of a play or a piece of art. The playgoer does not pay attention to the messages in the play hidden or overt, because of the slick lighting the body-vibrating sound, and the polished dialogue. We can see how drama allows itself to fall victim to style. One opening for critical pedagogy is to use style against itself.

Another aim for having drama in high schools, according to Motter, is to develop higher standards of public theatre. Educators hope that students will eventually demand higher artistic and cultural achievements in living theatre, motion pictures, and television. This concept of culture would seem to equate with what Herbert Marcuse (1978) called intellectual culture as opposed to material culture. Motter's book *Theatre in High School* (1970), while being a positive rationale for including drama in schools, needs to be more critical and accept the challenge of emancipatory critique and action. Teachers have to guard against playing into the manipulative hands of the culture industry. This creates a situation wherein people have to read a review before they know if they have enjoyed the play or not. We have to realize that the products of the culture industry should not be taken to represent given and eternal truths. It is dishonest to imply to students that what is offered, in popular theatre productions, always represents the best of the culture and society. Teachers should expose students to theatre that offers a critical perspective on the relationships between the individual and society and educate students to an awareness of the substantive nature of the theatre rather than allow students to be overcome by the trappings of theatre.

Dorothy Heathcote (1980) sees drama as helping in the pursuit of objectives not met by other methods. Heathcote's work is an attempt to expand student understanding of life experiences. She would have them reflect on a particular circumstance and seek to make deeper sense out of their world. Heathcote's method is to try to discover the tension and conflict of a given setting and then use its educative moment. Heathcote allows educational drama to project a situation that poses a dilemma and the drama unfolds as the dilemma is examined by those involved with the activity. In this approach Heathcote leaves room for the possibility of a critical drama pedagogy for she is willing to have students work problematic themes into a drama exercise. Heathcote may even be aware that the emancipatory effects of art are generated by the rejection of accepted forms of the dominant culture. She certainly feels free to examine presented forms of world order in her workshops and classes. Heathcote's work demonstrates that she sees schooling as rigidly organized, formalistic, and subject-centered rather than student-centered. This type of system rewards convergent thinking, acceptance of the status quo, passivity, and consensus. On the other hand a drama pedagogy that contains the principle of the emancipatory effects of art releases drama to recognize and indict these otherwise accepted practices. If such a procedure is allowed and encouraged, then cultural institutions as well as pedagogical practices can be demystified and left open to transformative action.

In her work Heathcote as a creative dramatist holds real promise for critical pedagogy for she puts great emphasis on reflection in drama. Yet Heathcote realizes that the material objects of the world give students a common source of knowledge (Bolton 1984). Drama makes use of that material world. I believe this notion offers a positive opening for critical pedagogy. The promise lies in working out a perspective that is both critical in thought and emancipatory in action.

We should consider Rosilyn Wilder's (1977) work when examining the problematic dimensions of culture, dominant rationality, social contradictions, and consciousness formation. Wilder suggests it is important for teachers to go beyond the positive reinforcement of students and help set up a pedagogy that dialectically treats the relationship of individuals to society. Students must want to change not only themselves but also the given reality that surrounds them. This will be a universal and seemingly endless struggle. Personal development is an essential step toward emancipatory critique and action; but if development ends with the individual, then it is difficult to imagine society at large developing and changing in an emancipatory fashion. We should not see personal development as the end of pedagogy.

To qualify for critical pedagogy, a drama program must go beyond the realms of student personal development and artistic performance. There must be an opportunity for students to see that their culture is a product, not only of the values of science, humanities, art, and religion, but also of the daily patterns of living such as leisure, education, and work. The fact that these patterns are problematic should not deter us from considering them within a critical pedagogy. Drama offers a unique site wherein such patterns can be freely examined.

The writing of Gavin Bolton (1979, 1984) is encouraging from the point of view of critical pedagogy. Bolton insists that drama in education must give attention not only to the crafts of the performer but also to the skills needed for a learning relationship to exist between teacher and student. Bolton sees drama in education as negotiation between students and teachers who are involved with a meaning making process. Drama in education, Bolton claims, is a process that focuses the thoughts and feelings of students on educational goals. Bolton would have drama in education as being more than the study of dramatic texts, more than the presentation of plays, and more than teaching about drama. In other words, drama in education goes beyond theatre and goes beyond its apparent self. We can appreciate the critical promise of Bolton's work when we see him encourage exploration and questioning as well as celebration of the human condition. Bolton who sees drama being used to challenge students' views and understandings would have drama involve the head, heart, and body. Perhaps most importantly, Bolton would set up a means to legitimate and encourage serious reflection within the drama. In this way the students can examine and build on their own knowledge, experiences, and cultural capital. This opportunity for empowered reflection is essential for a critical drama pedagogy. Fred Hawksley (1991) believes that one of Bolton's greatest contributions has been the elaboration of the teacher-in-role strategy, which allows the teacher to alter relationships with students and then greater meaning-making is achieved. When a teacher takes on a role in class, that teacher is, at least in a fictional sense, joining in with the class in the pursuit of a common objective. The teacher's agenda is different from the students'. The student may be content with being a fighter pilot in the Persian Gulf War, while the teacher may want to reflect on the social, historical, and economic forces that put the pilot in such a plane. For critical pedagogy the students have to get beyond the play. This sort of work calls for a delicate balance between teacher and student agendas. The temptation is to use the drama only for teacher objectives. In a very real sense the teacher-in-role is working through theatre. The teacher is using the elements of focus, tension, contrast, and symbol to do classroom drama work. As I have claimed before, it seems impossible to be a teacher-in-role without knowing and using the skills and form of theatre. The concept of teacher-in-role for critical pedagogy is most helpful.

> Such a device permits the integration of two modes that are normally thought of as incompatible: an existential, living through mode where the participants have some degree of autonomy over their experiencing and a theatrical mode that through use of tension, context, focus and symbolization heightens, sharpens and intensifies that experiencing. (Jackson 1980, 77)

Drama is not and cannot be immune from the normative interests behind schooling. However, if these interests are allowed to be examined as opposed to being simply accepted by teachers and students, then there is hope for transformative education. If such an approach is possible, then teachers can rescue drama in schools from its acritical grounding. Many drama models have lurking below their surfaces emancipatory possibilities. Teachers who are able to work from a position of critical pedagogy can redeem some of these models. This does not mean magic-time or prepackaged recipes for critical drama. A critical drama pedagogy will follow its own demands.

David Hornbrook claims that production and critical interpretations are all important in school drama (Male 1990). He would have students study the basic elements of dramatic art: space, sound, gesture, discourse, text, form, and mise-en-scene. Teachers can do this through the basic methodologies of improvisation, role play, script work, and technical training along with editing and performance analysis.

For Hornbrook (1989), the key term is dramatic art. This means everything from improvisation to published plays. He makes the very valid distinction between the production of original work and the reproduction of established texts. The way that production and reproduction are used in drama can be helpful in our understanding of the same salient terms from the critical theory literature. We produce plays when we are free to put our own interpretation and imprint on them; we reproduce plays in drama when we simply copy them. There is obviously a world of difference between the two processes, and making the distinction is crucial for critical pedagogy.

Hornbrook is also helpful in getting us beyond the notion of the playwright as a hidden isolated genius. Realizing that the playwright is not separate from society, Hornbrook sees the playwright as a producer within a society. He would put his students in the work of playwright, director, designer, and actor. There is great value for critical pedagogy in demystifying these roles. Hornbrook would want students to use dramatic art to examine the institutions and structures of society.

Hornbrook's understanding and uses of dramatic text are quite helpful.

> We may usefully describe the dramatic product, the outcome, that is, however provisional, of rehearsal, spontaneous improvisation or role playing, as a *dramatic text*. It is important to stress that this use of the word text allows it a wider application than that limited to written scripts. A text may indeed describe the script of a play but here it is extended to cover any form of active discourse or performance that can be *read* and *interpreted* by watchers. (1989, 105)

Using dramatic text in this way is most useful for critical pedagogy for it allows teachers to go beyond reproduction to production. Hornbrook's opinion of narratives is also quite helpful in any discussion of critical pedagogy. School drama must go beyond reinforcing past practices for individual social advancement. "While the art that evokes the most profound meanings for a society must be both reflective and critical of that culture, it cannot ever be historically in advance of the economic circumstances within which it is necessarily contained" (p. 107).

Hornbrook put much weight on what he calls narratives of historical consciousness. Claiming that such narratives help us understand, articulate, and transform our worlds, he is quick to point out that narratives must reflect and celebrate the diversity of students' cultural backgrounds. A critical pedagogy of drama can build on this positive opinion.

If we take a narrative approach to drama in our schools, then we have to let ourselves be open not only to the temporal dimensions of knowledge but also to moral, emotional, and aesthetic dimensions. We have to bring not only the cultural but the personal into drama (Connelly and Clandinin 1988).

Hornbrook suggests that a concept of dramatic art dissolves the distinction between drama and theatre. Even if that claim is not totally realized, it certainly is helpful. It is my contention that drama and theatre must dialectically contribute to each other. I believe it is much more helpful to see drama and theatre as two elements of the same body: the lead and the glass in a stained-glass window.

Built into this study is a belief that society contains unrealized possibilities. By its very form drama is open to explore beyond that which is given and accepted and provides a medium for critical thinking to the extent that it can hold up images of life that question and contradict the existing reality. Drama teachers must realize where drama fits into the process of cultural production and reproduction. It helps to remember that education often mystifies the process by which power relationships in society are reproduced in the classrooms, in the playgrounds, and on the drama stage. Drama can help students discover the possible within everyday things so that students can be free to interpret the possibilities for a richer existence embedded in the cultural tradition. Students must be free to work the various forms of drama that enable them to explore their worlds and plot their destinies. Drama in schools must be more than a reflection of social reality; schools must be free to show alternative visions of the relationships between the individual and society. Stuart Bennett (1984) reminds us that we have to place drama in its overall social context and remember that it is a cultural activity. The culture that we build on in our use of drama contains values as well as knowledge. The past cultural values embedded in a drama script may not be the values of students who work with such drama. If we understand culture as being something that is made, then we have some chance of separating ourselves from the values of the cultural past. Drama in education must place itself beyond mere transmission of knowledge and values.

Bennett builds on Paulo Freire's work when he insists that drama must be seen as a practice of freedom. We do not need drama primarily to answer questions for us. Drama can serve teaching better if it also helps ask the questions. The questions then serve as a dialectical tension that can trigger critical thinking.

Bennett reminds us of the great story from Augusto Boal (1979) who tells about the shoe-shine boys forced to rent a nail from a business owner to hang up their heavy shoe-shine boxes. For them the nail was a symbol of exploitation. In a critical drama pedagogy we have to help our students see the nails on the wall in our society. Like Bennett, we have to ask not what drama is but what it does. Much of what we do in school drama is apolitical. However, our lives are certainly political. We simply have to ask more questions about the lives we live and the human politics we support. In essence we have to do our bit to make culture.

Critical drama should not allow itself to fall victim to style. The drama teacher who is interested only in award-winning productions may well use style to achieve such ends. In doing so, the teacher will likely lose the transformative value of drama. Students working within drama should not allow themselves to surrender to the spectacle; instead, teachers must encourage them to accept the challenge to make sense of what they are seeing, hearing, and feeling. There must be more to drama than there is in seeing a fireworks parade at Disneyworld. Drama should be more than sensations—not that there is anything wrong with sensations. However, if part of our agenda is to work toward self and social transformation, our educational tools must have critical moments. In true critical drama the lights, sounds, and sets should point the way to dissonance, questioning, and critique of the drama form and meaning. Students of critical drama should not applaud actors whose gestures, emotions, and characters are mere extensions the their wardrobe and make-up.

A critical drama should help students examine their own life experiences through the reflective analysis of role playing and improvisation. The vision of life shown to students, through drama, could be presented against the social meaning systems of the students themselves. Drama should use its theatrical masks to reveal and free, not to hide and bind. At its best, a critical drama can make breaks with the dominant expectations of school and society. Drama must become, in the process of schooling, a movement toward a consciousness of what might be. In so doing drama can aid in bringing about needed social changes that through critical consciousness could result in a freer human development.

As I claimed a number of times during the development of this text, drama in its widest educational use remains flagrantly acritical. Often drama refuses to articulate an interest in individual and social transformative action. Drama rejects the challenge to treat dialectically the relationships between the individual and society. Often models of drama pedagogy concentrate on aims that treat the subject as object and in isolation. The student using drama is not always regarded as a subject within a culture that is in formation. I ground this text in the belief that things can change and those new possibilities within the lived experience can be envisioned and realized. Drama education need not be content with working solely on student development and producing entertaining plays. Drama education can take a critical interest in individual and social transformative action and help teachers see their role in a more critical perspective.

In an attempt to realize drama's critical needs I will, in the following section, bring the elements of critical theory to bear on the material presented in chapter three. I used chapter three of this study to give a necessary understanding and familiarity with traditional models of drama education. Covering a wide range of educational aims and practices, these models demonstrate the ambiguity of the drama field. Many of the models are united in their existence to critical pedagogy. Such models are uniform in their refusal to articulate an interest in individual and social emancipation and neither treat dialectically the relationships between the individual and society nor point to the promise of emancipatory critique and action.

The essence of drama is our interaction with the total environment and the struggle to understand the significance of the lived experience. Drama within education has undoubtedly been used in this task of understanding the lived experience. Both critical theory and drama seek to understand all forms of social practice that hinder self-consciousness and free development.

Drama from its conflict and dialogue develops argument and discourse. In this manner, drama allows for a distrust of claims to the reconciliation of contradictions. Such drama resists the temptation to resolve contradictions in a spurious harmony. By allowing argument and discourse, drama can show the contradictions of social reality in its own form and in its own structure. By using argument and discourse, the teacher through the drama works presented, bears witness to dialectical truth, and helps maintain the gap between subject and object as well as between individual and society.

It is not the intention of this text to dictate prescriptions for an emancipatory drama pedagogy. I would like again to reiterate Max Horkheimer's warning that there can never be a once-and-for-all formula that lays down the relationships between individuals and society. I agree with Henry Giroux's (1981) stance that such prescriptions are inconsistent with any viable theory of emancipation. In a real sense, any critical drama pedagogy will follow its own demands if left open to these demands. The very existence of recipes for a critical drama pedagogy would militate against the necessary open-ended philosophy called for by Horkheimer. If a critical drama pedagogy is to serve, beyond the usual packaging processes within schooling, it must itself be a model of freedom. A critical drama pedagogy must be open to its own critique.

Within the broad perspective of critical theory, as elaborated by the Frankfurt School, there is a search to understand the forms of social values, attitudes, and practices that hinder self-consciousness and free human development. Built into this search and standing behind it is a belief that society contains unrealized potentialities. Educators can use drama to point to those possibilities beyond the given sociohistorical reality. Drama, open to explore possibilities beyond what is given, provides a medium for critical thinking to the extent that it can hold up images of life that contradict the existing reality. If drama can hold up images of unrealized possibilities, it can also encourage men and women to work for their realization. People can come to know their unfreedom and in so doing break through petrified social reality. Students of drama cannot only develop as human beings in cocoon fashion but also act out their unfreedom and improvise other possibilities. If people can see the possibilities for living in a more self-conscious and free manner, they will strive for it. The human spirit is not necessarily pessimistic.

Teachers must realize that the drama programs they use may well be instruments that hinder self-consciousness and free development. Drama teachers can free themselves from such a burden by being critical of the program being used and by being aware of the inherent possibilities.

Drama educators must realize where drama fits into the process of culture and its production and reproduction. Drama teachers need to remember that culture is an expression of human consciousness that is shaped by social living. Often we relegate drama to that view of culture that refers only to the values of art within the humanities. This is what Marcuse refers to as intellectual culture. Drama gets much of its raw material from the daily patterns of behavior within the social psychological and moral dimensions of family, leisure, education, and work. Marcuse calls this material culture. Drama as an artifact of culture must relate to society in general. It is my contention that drama education suffers because public theatre is often limited to intellectual culture and becomes the property of the elite. And so drama often reflects the culture of the dominant group.

CULTURAL CAPITAL

It is imperative for a critical pedagogy of drama that educators be aware of the cultural capital of students. By cultural capital is meant the socially determined tastes, prior knowledge, language forms, abilities and modes of knowing that are held by students, as well as teachers, in varying degrees (Giroux 1981). Teachers need to be aware of this fact and to realize what culture is being indicated and transmitted within their drama programs. From my perspective, drama is a premier vehicle for cultural transmission. Drama has within it the means to put before its students the various tastes, knowledge, and language forms and indicate to them pre-ferred abilities as well as modes of knowing. We must realize drama in its educational use to be a powerful reproducer of existing modes of social relationships. In this, educational drama can be seen as a vehicle by which the powerless are made (albeit by consent) to accept their fate and perpetuate social inequality. Drama educators need to recognize the inherent worth of students' cultural capital and to accept and reinforce it. For that cultural capital is a reflection of human consciousness as it is shaped by a particular social living. The drama teacher who reinforces one student's cultural capital over another is doing an injustice to both of the students as well as cancelling the emancipatory possibilities of drama education. We must aim a critical drama pedagogy at both the oppressed and the dominant, at those who make up the rules and agendas as well as those who follow the rules and agendas. The dominant should realize that it is simply not right for a limited culture to be foisted on society as the only culture. Both the oppressed and the dominant could examine what is the value of calling one culture superior and another inferior.

It is important for educators to realize that drama, within the institution of the school, can be a means by which the culture of the dominant classes becomes the official culture. Teachers of drama should examine their own class style and accent so they can realize what culture they are exhibiting and reinforcing. Teachers may be very ineffective if they verbally express empathy for subordinate cultural production but bear the imprint of dominant cultural production. This is a complex problem for teachers. Can we teach students if we are not part of their culture or are unable to appreciate that other culture? Do teachers rework their own cultural capital to adapt to the cultural capital of their students? There is a real dilemma here for teachers. I believe teachers have to be authentic. Then they have to seek ways of going out from their own culture to accommodate students from another culture. This act calls for knowledge, patience, and pedagogical faith.

CRITICAL DRAMA

Educators, who would wish a critical drama pedagogy, need to realize that the emancipatory effects of drama are generated in large part by the rejection of dominant forms of world order. Drama must also demonstrate how powerful interests realize themselves through cultural phenomena. To do this, drama must become not only a vehicle of recognition of social inequalities but an indictment of those inequalities. Drama education, within its demystifying possibilities, must be celebration as well as indictment. Helping students see the possibilities within everyday living, drama can free students to interpret these possibilities for a freer and richer existence embedded in a given cultural tradition. To do this, drama must maintain its own freedom. Students must be free to work with various forms of drama to explore their world and express what could be their destiny. In a critical pedagogy, drama should not simply represent society. If drama is a mere reflection of social reality, it can have little emancipatory hope. The strength of drama is that it can show alternative visions of the relationships between the individual and society. If high school drama's only purpose is to portray real life, then we can't call it critical pedagogy. Drama must be free to call injustice, inequality, or horror by their names and be able to testify against them. The high school play or drama program that glosses over the unequal relationships within society is not living up to its transformative possibility. Drama can help break the monopoly of sociohistorical reality by pointing to the possible reality so that students can imagine and create this possible reality for themselves. Reality should not be merely accepted as a given by the drama teacher or the program planner; such people may well visualize another reality, another destiny.

Drama programs, in their design and execution, should not fall into the hands of a culture industry attempting to fuse the old and the familiar into a new quality. The success of such a culture industry depends on the unfreedom of the consumers. Teachers of drama must be aware of current fashion and not be content with merely following formulas to produce a hit play. Students of drama should see such a phenomenon for what it is worth. If a play can be standardized, then it could be expected to serve the cultural industry. In the least, it serves conformity and consensus. In this way, the products of the culture industry are taken to represent given and eternal truths. If the plays used in high schools are products of the cultural industry, then such plays may not be able to contribute to a critical pedagogy.

Teachers, in a critical drama program, should choose and develop plays that show the contradictions within society and do not attempt to solve conflicts only on the surface. Critical high school drama calls for a celebration of reason, sensitivity, and spontaneity. In the face of the conformity called for by the culture industry, drama teachers need to be autonomous, independent, and critical individuals. This does not mean that drama teachers do not have institutional constraints, but it may be the task of a critical educator to try to transform such constraints. In short the critical drama teacher should be a model for self-consciousness and free development.

Following on the Frankfurt School's idea of culture industry it seems important that a critical drama pedagogy needs to be aware of the place of style. We have to realize that style can be an impediment to any hoped-for critical pedagogy of drama for style is insidious to the extent that it can subsume the message as well as the content. Drama can captivate students by style and glitter; and such students, like adults, often remain acritical. Style allows the culture industry, as diffused as that industry might be, to administer culture.

It would seem that teachers interested in a critical drama pedagogy are able to control the influence of style. Teachers can help students to see style for what it really is: the ephemeral surface of the content. Teachers can point to the message and purpose of drama's form and help students see beyond the lighting, sound, and set design. It should be noted that light, sound, and set design can be authentic art forms in themselves, however, the warning here is against their use to subvert critical appraisal of the reality portrayed in a play. Critical drama should not allow itself to fall victim to style. Neither should style dictate or supersede the roles portrayed in a play, nor should the roles supersede or replace the message of a play. With fascination for style, drama may not treat dialectically the relationships between the individual and society nor point to the promise of emancipatory critique and action.

Critical drama pedagogy must show a distrust for claims to the reconciliation of contradictions that are found in many stage plays and movies. Critical drama must express the ideas of harmony negatively by embodying the contradictions of the lived experience pure and uncompromised. A successful drama form does not simply resolve contradictions in a spurious harmony but shows these contradictions in its own structure. Because drama uses space, color, sound, and movement, the possibility to play one against the other is almost limitless. Drama, especially in its theatre form, can show images of contradiction by matching cold light with a warm theme or by holding up symbols of oppression in a set that, on the surface, is meant to appear benevolent. Drama as a form of critical pedagogy must hold on to and demonstrate the relations and gaps between subjectivity and objectivity. Drama can remind students that there is a life between illusion and reality, falsehood and truth, as well as joy and death. If a teacher insists on happy endings and once-and-for-always solutions to social contradictions, then the drama program is not bearing witness to the dialectical truth of reality. We should regard drama, as Maxine Greene would claim, as a province of meaning. Critical drama should help students examine their own life experiences through the process of role playing, improvisation, and a critical analysis of plays presented to them.

The vision of life presented to the students through drama ought to be presented against the social meaning systems of the students themselves. Students must see the deficiencies as well as the possibilities of the world. Only in this way can teachers help students form a consciousness that may transform the lived experience. The perpetuation of ideal states, and the resolutions of contradictions in romantic harmony have no place in a drama pedagogy that would claim to be critical. Part of the search in this text is for a critical understanding that can empower drama to transform, even if in only some limited way. Greene (1990) claims critical understanding precedes freedom. However, teachers of drama should remind their students that art cannot fulfill the promise of emancipation on its own. Art, in its drama forms, must not promise Utopia, for art can only work through human agents toward emancipation.

Critical theory has given us the important ideas of affirmative art and negative art. In summary, affirmative art, which sees the entire sphere of material production as tainted by poverty, severity, and injustice, refuses any demands to protest that sphere. This form of art affirms the status quo as it sees it. It is important for critical drama to aid in the abolishment of affirmative art and the culture it represents. Critical drama must help subvert the dominant consciousness of the ordinary experience and protest the social relations, must not accept the poverty, severity, and injustice as a given part of the lived experience and must form part of a schooling process that provides liberating images and practices against affirmative culture. In this process, the Frankfurt School would call for negative art, that is, a drama form that protests the given sphere and shows alternatives. We should remember that a call for negative art is not a call for magic time. It is a call for what is possible. Negative images of the present sociohistorical reality are possible. Schooling practices that go against the status quo, with its dominant rationality are possible. Drama education can supply such images and initiate such practices. Drama, as I claimed earlier, is a premier vehicle for cultural critique and can live the promise of emancipatory critique and action.

In its most emancipatory moment, critical drama education can intervene actively in consciousness formation. Drama cannot of itself promise emancipation or transformation. Drama can, however, be an integral factor in shaping the quality and the appearance of things and of life. Drama within the schooling process cannot change the world but can point to a change in consciousness in people who can change the face of lived experience. Drama in its many forms while recognizing evil and pointing to the promise still must be a human agency that transforms the given society.

As Marcuse claims, drama can be an indictment of the established reality (Marcuse 1978). In this way drama in its pedagogical forms can help break the bond of destruction, suppression, and hegemonic control. Drama can show images and causes of destruction, can reflect suppression in its cause, can expose the rule of consent and indict it. At its best drama can point to change in the consciousness of human agents who can then refuse the rule by consent. In short, human agents can develop a critical consciousness (Freire 1981). Freire's idea of *conscientização* is helpful here for it speaks of learning to perceive social, political, and economic contradictions and to take action against oppressive elements of reality. This concept does not stop at the level of subjective perception of a situation. Emancipatory action prepares us for the struggle against the obstacles to humanization. Drama education in its critical format must learn to respond to students as particular people in particular conditions. Critical drama must dispense with stereotype roles, easily solved conflicts, and no-choice options. In this way drama can mask reality. Drama, instead, should use its theatrical masks to reveal and free, not to hide and bind. Drama must make critical understanding possible to the sources of sense-making and open new ways of coming in touch with the social self (Greene 1980). If drama presents aspects of the world with its deficiencies and injustices and moves against them in a manner that shows not only emancipatory critique but also action, then we are well on our way to a form of critical pedagogy.

At its best a critical drama pedagogy can make breaks with dominant expectations and alienate the familiar. Drama must become, in the process of schooling, a tool toward a consciousness of what might be. In so doing drama can aid in bringing about needed changes, that through critical consciousness, could result in freer human development.

5

A Site for Critical Pedagogy

Dysart: The thing is, I'm desperate. You see, I'm wearing that horse's head myself. That's the feeling. All reined up in old language and old assumptions, straining to jump clean-hoofed on to a new track of being I only suspect is there. I can't see it, because my educated, average head is being held at the wrong angle.

Peter Shaffer, *Equus*

My plan in this chapter is to present a number of scripted plays and design suggestions that testify how critical theory can be used in a critical drama pedagogy. Further to this, I wish to indicate how relevant themes from student experiences can be worked through dramatic play in a manner that can be part of cultural production. First, it is useful for us to have some sense of what is possible with student drama.

Jack Zipes, writing about German children's theatre, claims that:

German children have been given a steady diet of banal, cute plays diluted of reality in order to distract them from their real oppressive surroundings and to keep them unaware of how they might use their wits and initiative to develop their potentialities and possibly change society. (1976, 1)

Harsh as this statement is, the underlying sentiment is most instructive. Part of the challenge for a critical pedagogy of drama is to take the world of students seriously. This drama should move toward greater collectivity and equality. We have to realize that the drama produced for and by students is drama about society at large. The problems and promise of students are the problems and promise of society. The aim of critical drama should be to offer possible alternatives rather than final solutions. It is more important to encourage dialectical thinking than to produce entertaining plays or merry tragedies. Critical drama should be praxis in the full sense of the word: a place to act out reflective theory.

It is my thesis that we do not always have to invent new plays to contribute to a critical pedagogy of drama. There are many openings for the production of new plays, but there are also in circulation many scripted plays that offer transformative moments. Much of what I am suggesting for a critical drama pedagogy has less to do with new content than it has to do with looking at existing content with new eyes.

Stuart Bennett (1984) writes about students making their own culture. This is going way beyond seeing theatre as a received practice with all its forms and rituals in place. Here I am talking about cultural production. Bennett believes this process to be primarily an act of communication and endorses Boal's practice of presenting audiences with an unfinished play. The author invites the audience to continue the play giving their own conclusion. Of course Boal would say the play is never finished. We do not have to treat scripted plays as finished either. For purposes of critical pedagogy, students can write a third act for a two-act play. What happens to Chief, in *One Flew Over the Cuckoo's Nest,* after he runs away from the psychiatric institution? How does Shirley Valentine act when her formerly dominant husband appears on that Greek beach? Did Dysart, in *Equus,* ever break the chains of social conformity that were holding him down? This is the type of question that can be explored in working beyond a given script for a critical drama program.

Bennett believes that the techniques and skills of theatre give us the tools to work with in drama; these tools of theatre can be focusing and precise. Teachers use the tools of theatre to help students build their own drama and in turn enable them to produce their own culture. Part of what I would like to do in this chapter is to examine some well known play scripts in a search for their critical moments. The intent is to extract these critical moments in a way that allows students and teachers to produce their own meanings out of someone else's script. The search here is for emancipatory openings and not the reinforcement of great literature. I will examine the scripts for opportunities of self-empowerment and social transformation. After all, these scripts are filled with experience, history, and vested interest and as such are fruitful material for critical pedagogy. Greene (1990) reminds us that scripts are not invented from thin air:

> Human beings, of course, devise their life projects, in time, against their own life histories, and the wider human history into which those histories feed. . . . To be aware of authorship is to be aware of situationality and of the relation between the ways in which one interprets one's situation and the possibilities of action and of choice. This means that one's "reality," rather than being fixed and predefined, is a perpetual emergent, becoming increasingly multiplex, as more perspectives are taken, more texts are opened, more friendships are made. (p. 23)

In a critical pedagogy we have to get away from the idea that playwriting is done only in isolation by the gifted few. Drama production is a group form. Playwriting can be an extension of students' playing. We have to help students make their own drama not merely accept uncritically someone else's theatre. One of the other myths we need to battle is that students should only be involved with limited aspects of drama. In particular I am suggesting that students can do more than act and can be more than foot soldiers of school drama. They can direct, write, and design. Too often a teacher chooses and directs a drama exercise, project, or play. The students have little choice but to live out the agenda of the teacher. The teacher "does" the play; the students merely act it out. This strategy is limiting for students. The final public presentation, if there is one, might be more polished and entertaining, but it could remain empty as far as the students are concerned. One of the first moves toward a critical drama pedagogy is to give ownership of the dramatic play back to the students. This certainly does not mean that the teacher steps away from the dramatic play but that the teacher works in a collaborative mode with students rather than in top-down isolation. We do not need research literature to tell us that as humans we learn best when we are engaged in our study and when the object of our study attracts and holds our attention. Theodore Sizer (1991) tells us teachers rather than the students do the work. Teachers present the material and students display back what they have been exposed to. Teachers need to engage students. Sizer goes on to claim that "we must change the curriculum from a display-of-content to questions-that-ultimately-provoke-content. Press the kids to do the work, to solve the problems presented. The cost? It takes longer to provoke kids to learn for themselves than it does to deliver content to them" (p. 33).

Drama teachers can attempt many of Sizer's recommendations to help students look at the raw material of their lived culture and drawing from this material, interpret it for themselves and for others. They can also be encouraged to probe the history of a given shared community experience and build on that history examining it for its moments of repression and resistance. All this can be played out in dramatic form in a way that produces a living text although not necessarily a written one. It can be a structure for improvisation or storytelling. One may or may not have a performance.

I am taking a simple approach between drama and theatre. For my purpose here theatre is drama on stage. This working distinction allows us the freedom to use drama, in its widest sense, to begin building a critical pedagogy. In other words, the total world of drama is at our disposal. Those who regard live theatre as the only true form of drama are comparable to those contemporaries of Gutenberg who would acknowledge only a hand-written book as a true book. Through the mass media, drama has become one of the most powerful means of communication between human beings. It is far more powerful than the printed word, which was the basis of the Gutenberg revolution (Esslin 1978).

We need to examine drama, which is a given in our students' lives and culture. Student culture fills the drama of movies, rock videos, and hang-outs. Students "hang out" in dramatic clusters in shopping malls, hamburger restaurants, and school washrooms. Moving in discrete packs they seek drama with a shout here or an encounter there. Students make up this dramatic play as they move inside rituals of resistance and loyalty. Their dramatic play should not go unattended and unexamined. Inherently dramatic, this play is the stuff of their lives.

In drama we have to watch for many things. Drama can be a trap for teachers and students for its is easy to get caught up in the applause of a fine dramatic presentation. There is nothing wrong with liking applause. It is only amiss if the applause is the prime reason for doing drama. We should not be afraid of silence. Even though the sound of no hands clapping can be unnerving, the drama can still be transformative. We must not confuse enjoyment with understanding. People still want to know. I believe one good question can justify an otherwise merely entertaining play. There is little value in showing people what they already know. Instinctively an audience seeks a play that reinforces the status quo. We all want to believe what we already believe. Yet, we know from experience that happy or unrealistic endings leave us empty. With happy or unrealistic endings, we can leave the play behind us in the theatre building. However, if there is a question or a pointed finger, we might leave a little more puzzled. Drama should not be afraid of ambiguity. Members of an audience want their experiences to count for something, and these life experiences of the audience are the links with the students' play. This is not a question of giving people what they want, but of making their experiences count.

SCRIPTED PLAYS

The intent of working with existing texts is "to provide teachers and students with the critical tools necessary to analyze those socially constructed representations and interests that organize and emphasize particular readings of curriculum materials" (Giroux 1989, 138). One of the strongest emancipatory clues for drama pedagogy is to appreciate how scripts can be produced in such different fashion; that is, no two presentations of a play are the same. Drama is forever new. Because drama is multidimensional, scripts can be interpreted in many ways. Directors can decide to emphasize one aspect over another. A drama script does not have to be frozen. Often established scripts are removed from their original settings and made to comment on a world better known to the director, actors, and audience. The new reading or presentation cannot pretend that the context is the same as the one that fostered the original play. Scripts must be open to rereading. Of course, the new reading, or presentation, must then be made open to critique. The new reading or presentation is no more free from history, ideology, or politics than was the original. Making a script our own does not free it from social influences. Just as the original script was written from the cultural material of its time, so the new must be read and seen within the present cultural context. The very adaptation is loaded with social ideology. Yet, it remains a powerful tool of inquiry. A drama script can serve as an educational grid for examining different social, cultural, and political contexts. David Hornbrook's concept of dramatic text is helpful here. He reinforces the idea that a play is not written in isolation and separate from society. The writer of the play, which students are grappling with, works from inside a culture.

When teachers and students are working with scripted plays, they need to look at the social inequalities that might lie under the surface of relationships between characters. The temptation is to simply say "that is the way it was at the time." If teachers take that approach, emancipatory moments may be lost. It is too simple to say that Shylock, in *The Merchant of Venice*, was treated in a negative way because of historical ethnic prejudice, and not realize that there are many similar contemporary examples.

Equus

From any point of view, *Equus* is a most powerful play. Peter Shaffer (1973) claims that his impetus for the play came from reading in a local newspaper about a real life account concerning a boy who blinded horses. It also seems to be a scripted play that allows the drama teacher to search for moments of understanding and transformation that can be used, in a dialectical fashion, with students. *Equus* tells the stories of two very different protagonists who are welded together through the bond of being psychiatrist and patient. The psychiatrist, Martin Dysart, is unfulfilled and the patient, Alan Strang, has blinded horses found in a stable. One questions the psyche, and the other answers in commercial jingles. Dysart seeks to find out all the pertinent factors that caused the teenager to go berserk. This search leads to knowledge about parental incompatibility, religious fixation, and unconsummated love. Alan, throughout his fixation, has turned the stable into a temple of horse-gods with staring eyes. However, in his failure, the gods had to be destroyed.

In this play Shaffer shows some anger at the well-ordered world he sees around him. This expressed anger is a window for teachers and students to peel back the layers of civilization they see around them. They get to examine the relationships between doctor and patient, doctor and nurse, parent and parent, as well as between doctor and parent. These relationships, based on power and knowledge, are lived out in expressions of fault, blame, and guilt. Blatant questions about life values are laid bare in this scripted play. For example, Dysart struggles to make Alan normal while asking what is normal. Open questions like this challenge students and teachers.

While scrutinizing *Equus*, teachers and students have many ways of approaching it critically. For example, teachers can invite students to work outside the play. Following this method, students might be asked to interview the psychiatrist. Students would, of course, use their own questions. Perhaps they could form a hospital committee to decide what sort of treatment would best help Alan. Students could write a report detailing what sort of personal and social pressure may have contributed to Alan's horrible act or they could dramatically improvise sharing a hospital room with Alan Strang. Throughout these exercises, students deal with a central question of who is responsible not only for Alan but for all of us. In such work, they are also producing dramatic text of their own.

One of the central symbols of this play is the chain used in the horse's mouth. Shaffer also applies this chain to Dysart's life. Can it be applied to ours? What forms of chains shackle our lives? What symbols can the students suggest and construct that would signal freedom for Dysart and Alan? What are their own symbols of freedom?

The Ecstasy of Rita Joe

The Ecstasy of Rita Joe is scripted by George Ryga (1971) who writes about Indians and laborers and is concerned with the problem of individual integrity. Ryga writes lyrically about realistic situations. His plays are filled with images and music that dance to themes of nature, turmoil, and resistance. A poet rather than a dramatic technician, he peppers his dialogue with symbolism and dissonance. Ryga's plays are filled with flashbacks, foreshadowings, and digressions. In fact, Ryga's work is a form of oral art that makes use of storytelling and song writing and uses dance as a symbol of the joy of life.

Ryga has a great feeling for the commonplace. He tries to write about the realities of this time as he understands them. It is difficult, he realizes, to accomplish understanding on a continent that is short on myth, ritual, and ceremony.

Ryga, whose main interests are ethical, writes of the harsh realities of existence. In an introduction to *The Ecstasy of Rita Joe* Brian Baker tells us that the playwright is primarily interested in the lives of rural and urban poor, what he calls the "stunted strong." In Ryga's work people are judged by their concern for individuals, and the playwright is scathing about impersonal welfare and justice.

Striving for the principle of parenthood in his characters, Ryga urges the acceptance of responsibility for the family as well as for society. He writes against the use of impersonal rules and demoralizing charity.

Ryga offers a direction for the critical educator when he does not wish to offer answers to the questions he raises. There is often tyranny in correct answers. Correct answers are often the tools of educational hegemony. Ryga's work consigns great raw material for a critical drama pedagogy. In dialectical fashion he holds up the empty lives of the dispossessed against the natural beauty of human dignity. Critical pedagogy finds a place wedged between such polarities.

The Ecstasy of Rita Joe is a play about the despair of Native Americans. It focuses on one individual, Rita Joe, in a way that informs us about the whole of society. In doing this the play tries to get behind "the protective shutters of civilization" (p. xiii). This is a story about a young woman, lost in a white world, struggling for family, dignity, and justice. Surrounded by uncaring surrogate parents who rely on rules to make her conform, she is expected to reject her culture and become just another ingredient in the melting pot. But Rita Joe will not conform and the quest for integrity becomes fatal. For Rita Joe, this search becomes self-destructive. In the final scene Rita Joe's death by rape is contrasted with a soft ballad. Brecht would smile.

As I have just indicated, *The Ecstasy of Rita Joe* is a helpful play for critical educators who use drama in their work. How can teachers make the best use of this play? On two occasions in the play, the audience is directly blamed for the plight of Native Americans. Here is an opportunity for students to respond to the charge. What would happen if the play was stopped at that point?

With whom would the students identify? Would they see themselves as being part of the oppression? What would be their real identity? What would be their responsibility? In practice what scenes could they produce that would provide a response to the blame? It would seem difficult not to respond in some fashion to such blame.

In *The Ecstasy of Rita Joe* there is an attempt to draw the audience into the heroine's thought processes, to show them the confusion in her mind between the past and the present. Which is more real for Rita Joe? Would the students see value in Rita Joe's past? Is her past an illusion as far as the students are concerned? What text could students produce to value or devalue Rita Joe's past? How could they produce text, written or improvised, to contrast her past with her present? This is a play that makes great demands on an audience but one that gives them something to go home with. Students must also have something to take home with them. How does Rita Joe speak to them? What aspects of their lives can be contrasted with Rita Joe's? What moments of emancipation are there for Rita Joe? How would individual students handle Rita Joe's life differently? These are questions for a critical drama pedagogy.

The Ecstasy of Rita Joe carries a strong message for all of us. On one level it helps all North Americans to understand a little better what the native peoples suffer in our society. Chief Dan George, in talking about *The Ecstasy of Rita Joe*, claimed it is "useless for people to hear if they do not listen with their hearts. Rita Joe helps them listen with their hearts—and when hearts are open, ears can hear" (Ryga 1971, 35). There is much to hear in this powerful play.

One of the more telling pieces of dialogue in the play is heard from the magistrate when he informs Rita Joe that nobody is a prisoner. Working from inside the script, students will be able to comment on that claim. What forms of prison are Rita Joe and her friends subjected to? Are there moral and social prisons as well as iron ones? Are students familiar with any of these prisons? If so, what are the possibilities for liberation? Students can put the script aside and produce their own moral, social, and material prisons. Who keeps them confined in such prisons? Who holds the keys to such prisons?

One of the realities shown in this play is the way white people leave clothes for the Indians to take. Here is an opening for students to role play a family at home gathering clothes for distribution to a native center. What clothing are they willing to give away? What would the dialogue be? What are the values evident in their discussions? In contrast students could step out of that role and step into the roles of people lining up to be given the donated clothing. What would they choose? What would their comments be? How would they feel? Is it possible that some would not accept the charity clothing? What would be their options? Is there hope beyond the charity lines? How is that hope generated and sustained?

One of the most telling images of the play comes from the stage directions in which the teacher and the magistrate use the same podium. A powerful image to convey the judgmental role of the teacher, this also speaks to the power of drama to educate by symbol and metaphor. The teacher explains to Rita Joe that when you put copper and tin into a melting pot, it comes out bronze. The teacher claims it is the same with people. However, she is quick to tell Rita Joe that the young Native American never will be bronze because she has come from nowhere and is going no place. In so doing this the teacher is disallowing the Native American culture and negating Rita Joe's past. It is easy to see why the future is in doubt because there is a strong link between our histories and our futures. *The Ecstasy of Rita Joe* can serve as a metaphor for how we can offend students' histories and experiences.

Rita Joe's boyfriend, Jamie Paul, claims that in the city they never learned his name. This may be the greatest disaffirmation of all. Jamie Paul demands that the magistrate give him back his truth. He wants to be taught who he really is and blames the system for taking his knowledge about himself away. He wants that knowledge back so he can live like a man. Jamie Paul shouts that white society wants the Indians to stay proud as long as they don't ask for their rights. This is a loud cry for authenticity. No person could ask for less. There is an opening here for critical pedagogy to ask students what Jamie Paul was missing. There is a further opening for teacher and students to produce a text that might suggest, in dramatic form, how Jamie Paul can be given back his integrity. What have students or their parents lost by way of integrity? How can the suggestions made for Jamie Paul and Rita Joe be applicable to the students involved in the drama?

Shirley Valentine

Shirley Valentine, by Willy Russell (1988), is the story of a housewife living in Liverpool, England. She is a woman who finds a way to reclaim her former self, and escape the daily discussions she has with her kitchen wall. The appeal of *Shirley Valentine*, lies in the unabashed exploration of female experience and its sensitive portrayal of the little compromises, trade-offs, and personal appeasements that can undermine the very core of womanhood, identity, and self. Shirley Bradshaw must regain her old self. She has, once again, to become Shirley Valentine. The moral domination by her husband has left Shirley a poor excuse of her authentic self. She is caught in the trap of minding for her husband and children and forgetting her own life. Her very existence has become a mere satellite of their world. How can she transform this life of hers?

Shirley escapes her "little life" by literally leaving the country. However, the real break comes from remembering her old self and in getting enough courage to accept an invitation to go to Greece. The transformation is within herself. Her going to Greece is simply the acting out of that self-empowerment. Once Shirley decides to go to Greece, she begins to find her voice. She becomes Shirley Valentine. Now she can chart new waters and expand her horizons.

As far as critical pedagogy is concerned. *Shirley Valentine*, is a useful vehicle of inquiry. This play deals with problems of personal and social power relations and as such gives students many opportunities to explore and analyze the forces acting upon Shirley's life.

These forces are often not far removed from the forces acting upon the lives of teachers and students. In other words, these forces are real. In act one of *Shirley Valentine*, the character has little sense of her own subjectivity or confidence in the value of her experiences. She has been allowing herself to be turned into an object. In a very real way, she has to go out and discover her subjectivity. She needs to have experiences that speak to her as a woman and as an authentic person. Students will be able to improvise parallel texts for *Shirley Valentine*. They will be able to walk and talk with Shirley as she works through her daily rituals as a housewife. With Shirley they can quiz her habits of servitude, her dedication to nonfulfilling tasks, and her willingness to suffer verbal and moral abuse. Through improvised interviews with Shirley, they can attempt to peel away the layers of social assumptions that expected her to be so accepting of her lot. What ideological forces positioned her role so clearly in front of her?

In using the fiction about Shirley Valentine, teachers must enable students to articulate their understandings of the world around them. For many students, Shirley Valentine could be the lady down the street or in the kitchen of their own house. The dramatic text, generated by students, does not have to be fictionally linked to Shirley whose story could simply be an echo of a life they know only too well. Here is an opportunity for students to examine their own stories. Their stories not analyzed, may remain at the level of stories and not serve as a basis for critical reflection. In a critical drama pedagogy there needs to be a place for structured reflection. It is the responsibility of the teacher to allow, structure, and expect such reflection. Students need to clearly understand their own experiences and social reality because they are the ones who can transform their lives.

In this play students can see how Shirley Valentine becomes a critical agent. One of the real values of *Shirley Valentine* for a critical pedagogy of drama is that she is transformed over the period of the play. She is not made perfect, just transformed. Through this fiction students can be helped to realize that transformation is a process and not a product. Transformation may never be complete. Yet, it is possible to become autonomous, independent, and life critical.

Duet for One

Duet for One, a scripted play by Tom Kempinski (1981), has two characters. Stephanie Abrahams is a world renowned violinist, who has developed multiple sclerosis and a wicked disposition. Dr. Alfred Feldmann is a German psychiatrist described as "typical." The action for the entire play takes place in Dr. Feldmann's consulting room.

Stephanie is striking, ambitious, aggressive, rich, confident, courageous, and in despair. She is seated in an electric wheelchair, which she uses as a weapon. Feldmann, who is dedicated, feeling, and wise, loves his work, the arts, and life. The whole play revolves around the professional relationship of these two people as Stephanie tries to come to grips with her physical condition. The conflict for Stephanie is quite obvious. She is a world renowned concert violinist who can no longer play the music she loves. Through her struggle Feldmann begins to wonder about his own life.

Throughout the process Stephanie is left dangling by Feldmann as he tries to force out her thoughts and feelings. The process is painful. Stephanie believes she has to make the adjustment from performing her art to finding a new life for herself. Initially, she makes plans to teach, to help her husband with his career, and to live. In a short while she begins to realize that teaching young children to play and helping her husband is simply not enough. But she cannot do more. She is trapped. What is the nature of this trap? She tells her psychiatrist that from the beginning music has meant everything to her, now it is gone. She takes her anger out on Feldmann. He has probed her insecurity about life without music and about her marriage. He even suggests she is envious about her husband's career as a composer.

Part of Stephanie's discussion with Dr. Feldmann has to do with her father's early attitude toward her music. Because he saw the music as a little girl's hobby. She had to struggle with her father to pursue her music. Being a businessman he simply could not see the value of making a career out of music. Music could not be taken seriously. He wanted more for his daughter. In order for Stephanie to be a career musician, she had to fight the dominance of her father. His view of the world was not her view. Stephanie knew where she was going. But in the final analysis, determination could not change her physical condition. In time she gives her violin away. She begins to doubt if she really has talent. Feldmann believes she will commit suicide. He wants her to fight, to seek out new, real possibilities. He suggests that the dedication she once gave to her violin, she should now give to herself. The ending of the play is inconclusive. Stephanie reiterates that music is her life while Feldmann suggests another session for the following week.

Duet for One gives the teacher positive openings to work, in a critical fashion, with students in a drama program or project. In this scripted play teachers can find the themes of domination and struggle. Questions of personal goals and independence are evident. There are also dialectical opportunities to dissect examples of personal relationships such as the one between Stephanie and her father. There are also opportunities to probe examples of professional relationships as realized between Dr. Feldmann and Stephanie. The whole critical debate about the relative value of types of knowledge and professions can center around the different view Stephanie and her father had of music and its place in the professional world.

Students, in small groups if necessary, could go outside the script to role play a scene between Stephanie and her father as they discuss her future. The role playing can be open-ended. Here would be an opportunity for the students to reflect on the value of certain types of work and articulate this value. They could also express what they would be willing to do to follow their own dreams. The struggle for self-determination would not have to be limited to the place of music in the work world. In an improvisational situation any dream would do. Here is an opening for students to be treated as critical agents. They could be encouraged to script with different restrictions a parallel play that could use other people trying to fight for what they believe in. In this way students could bring their own histories, experiences, and culture into the dramatic process. As the drama process is played out, the teacher could have the students step out of role to reflect on the personal and social significance of their improvised dialogue. The students and teachers could negotiate conventions to open and close the drama. For example, the teacher could signal that when the violin is placed on the table it is time for reflection and shared insights. Students can invent their own signals for similar occasions.

Building on *Duet for One*, students could generate a new ending. Certainly the story told in this play does not end. The group involved in working with the play could write a sequel. What would happen if Stephanie's multiple sclerosis went into medical remission? How does her father feel about her being able to play again? Would she want to see Dr. Feldmann again? Would he have any real interest in her after her treatment? Would he go to her concerts? What would be the nature of their relationship after the concert? This could be compared to their relationship when she came to his office. What in Feldmann's culture would have made him appreciate music? His appreciation for music could be compared with the lack of appreciation shown by Stephanie's father. There is an interesting opportunity here to scrutinize whose culture gets affirmed. As this new play is produced students would move back and forth between their own worlds, the fictional world improvised in their drama, and the scripted play. The teacher could create a dialectical relationship between these worlds. Thus, the two worlds of reality and fiction inform each other.

Is there a language of hope and possibility in *Duet for One*? What do students read as possibility? At the very end of the play Dr. Feldmann invites Stephanie to come back for more sessions. Is that a sign of hope? Is this a statement of possibility?

Children of a Lesser God

Children of a Lesser God, a play by Mark Medoff (1980), takes place in the mind of James Leeds. The characters and events "step from his memory" (p. 8). The set is designed to allow free movement of the play's characters. American Sign Language (ASL) is used in conjunction with verbal language. It is of interest to note that the playwright insists that the roles of Sarah, Orin, Dennis, and Lydia be performed by hearing impaired actors. This is as it should be.

In a truly literal sense this play is about voice. As such, it offers many opportunities for the critical drama teacher to work quite directly with students on the concept of voice. In many ways this text is about voice and shows how educators can help students find their own voices.

In the story line of this play, Sarah Norman has quite deliberately not learned to speak verbally. Having chosen to live out her life in a nonverbal way, Sarah seems content with using ASL for her communication. James Leeds, a new instructor at the school for the hearing impaired where Sarah does domestic work, is not content with the fact that she refuses to learn to speak. He knows she is very bright and believes he can help her. It is only later that he realizes that he should work with her. He has no doubt that she should learn to speak. He simply cannot comprehend why anyone would choose silence. Sarah believes that Leeds does not want to help her as much as he wants to change her. However, she does not want to be changed and she accuses him of speaking for her when she wants to speak for herself. In a real sense the play is about his acceptance of her right not to learn verbal language. It is about her right to choose whatever life she wants for herself.

Leeds begins with the assumption that everyone should be verbal. It takes him most of the play to question this assumption. His working life is dedicated to helping hearing impaired people speak verbally. In many ways he is successful with this task. However, Sarah wants to be left alone to work in isolation. She strongly resents that she always had to learn verbal language and that other people were not willing to learn sign language. They both have to realize that neither one of them has a monopoly on normal. Ultimately they have to meet somewhere in between silence and sound.

Children of a Lesser God holds a solid message for teachers who have to realize that respect for the consciousness and culture of their students is paramount. The task of the teacher is to create learning situations where students can articulate their understanding of the world. The articulation of this understanding must be in the student's own voice whatever that voice might be. This play, if used in a critical fashion, can also help students respect each other's voices. As educators we have to admit that students are often seriously oppressed by other students. Given the spheres of oppression that exist in our society, we should not be surprised by this claim. If students can be helped to realize that the oppression they inflict on others is a representation of the wider society, they might be able to see the evil more clearly. As Sarah claims, all have a right to speak for themselves.

In *Children of a Lesser God* there is a direct and clear connection between language and power. Without verbal language Sarah is powerless in a community that values verbal skills so much. She is quite literally silenced. The fact that she chooses this isolation does not alter the fact of the silence. She operates on the fringe of her community. Leeds, in some sense, wants to give her power. The problem initially is that he does not respect her personhood. Once she knows that he appreciates her subjectivity, she is much freer. There is freedom in acceptance.

Students can make use of this play to examine the politics of certain cultural forms. They can dialectically examine the script for the moments of resistance shown by Sarah, explore the social cost of that resistance, and probe the dramatic tension between Sarah and James as they both seek to direct her life through a specific mode of communication. What is more important is that students can work inside the script to seek out the possibilities for Sarah and James to affirm each other. We can do this by using a type of dramatic interjection; that is, the teacher or any of the students could stop the script and suggest a segment of text that would speak to personal empowerment for Sarah and understanding for James. The students could move outside the script and produce text, written or improvised, that would show Sarah as a critical agent. How would they act themselves if they were in similar positions? The teacher could change the context of the dramatic piece and allow students to operate in a community with some impairment comparable to Sarah's, for example the impairment could be visual. What constraints does society put on a blind person who refuses to read braille? How can we help them? Can students in role try to change that person?

The students, while working in small groups, could put themselves in a situation similar to Sarah's. They could physically impair themselves while in role, by using a means to prevent themselves from hearing, seeing, or talking. We can do this simply with ear plugs, bandages, and binding. The important thing is for students to get a sense of the impairment and then look for openings for empowerment from inside that impairment. This would help make the drama more authentic. What resources could the students draw on from their own backgrounds that would help them cope with the impairment and the social reality that goes with it?

Teachers would have to realize that the cultural capital that such students, in class or in role, bring to school might be very different from their own culture or from the school culture. Teachers would have to work to extend the perimeters of acceptable cultural capital, so that such marginalized students are made whole. As far as the students are concerned, friends are the most important part of schooling. Students find their own oasis of friends in school. If we are to respect that fact, we have to help students realize the social needs of all students. That includes students who are impaired or disadvantaged by poverty or lifestyle. *Children of a Lesser God* offers such openings.

The Flight of the Earls

The Flight of the Earls is a strikingly dramatic piece by Christopher Humble (1984). The action revolves around the Earl family in County Tyrone, Ireland. The internment policy by the government of Northern Ireland is a historical fact. In this process, hundreds of people were held, in some cases for up to two years, without trial.

Against this backdrop the playwright presents a family whose male members are covertly involved with the outlawed Irish Republican Army. Their fight for the cause is all consuming in its scope and intensity. This is in opposition to the women of the household, who strive to retain some semblance of normalcy.

In many ways Brigitte Earl is the catalyst for the play's rising action. Her realization, that her husband is capable of killing even her own brother for his cause, makes her see the horror of their personal and political lives. Pushed to her breaking point, she will no longer accept her husband's deceit without question.

In many ways the Earls are representative of Irish families throughout Northern Ireland. The tragic part of this story is that this one family could represent any family during the internment period or any family in Northern Ireland since before the Earls of Tyrone and Tyconnel fled their land in 1607.

The personal, social, historical, and political context of this play can serve as a wealth of material for a critical drama pedagogy. In a very overt way *The Flight of the Earls* deals with significant questions. These questions are begging to be dealt with in a dialectical fashion.

One of the universal and unresolved political debates has to do with the practice of internment in times of political crisis. The notion of internment is not a new one. In North America we have a long standing history of placing native peoples on reserves and of confining people of Japanese and German background to World War II "prisoner" camps. We can refine our notion of Indian reservations by referring to Nazi Germany's handling of the Jewish people. Internment is seen by many governments as a last resort because it offends everyone concerned by revoking civil rights and provoking public backlash. *The Flight of the Earls* is just one play dealing with internment as it has been executed in Northern Ireland.

Teachers and students can see this play as an indictment of a political way of life. We can use the play to point out how civilian mad bombers and soldiers with permission to shoot on sight cause such horror. In a sense, this play can serve as a microcosm for all that is violent in our world. Part of the challenge in dealing with this play is to analyze the social and political factors that historically cause such conditions. The politics of blame does not do much to explain the present horror. Students, in collaboration with their teachers, can place this story in any historical decade over the last four hundred years. Students could then see if the existing dialogue and storyline would stand the test of being placed in the circumstances of the past. Would attitudes, values, and practices travel over time? How different essentially are the power relations today as compared to other historical decades? What power did people have over their own lives? Who controlled the labor market and therefore the livelihood of people?

Students again could go outside the script to improvise or write their own version of events. Any play limits itself in the time and circumstances it represents. Students involved in a critical drama process do not have to be so limited. They can write scenes that can be sandwiched between existing scenes from the published script. They can improvise or write scenarios that elucidate what actually happens on stage. In *The Flight of the Earls*, Michael sends his wife's brother Timothy off with a bomb that is meant to kill him. Students could improvise or write a monologue in which Michael grapples with the decision to commit such a drastic deed. Here would be an opportunity to investigate Michael's motives and values. Students could also play the role of Timothy, as he carries the deadly nail bomb on the bus. Is he suspicious? Does he realize he has been used before to carry bombs and leave them to explode in the faces of innocent people? Teachers can use this fiction to inspect the social and economic conditions that breed such desperation. Students could play the roles of the people in the play, as they wait in line to be hired for a day's work. The teacher could play the role of the hirer, who is selecting men and women to work in the shipyards. What are the motives of this person? Does the hirer allow a person's religious background to influence the choice? The teacher can then step out of role and set the scene in a factory or building site that would be familiar to the students. Now the teacher is in role as a local factory boss and the students play themselves as adults. They have the responsibilities of home and family. Now it is difficult for them to get jobs because of religion, color, or gender. How does lack of steady work manifest itself in the home? The scene is around the dinner table with the students in role as bread winners. What are the conditions of their invented lives? How do such lives compare to the bread winners in *The Flight of the Earls*? In this way teachers and students move in and out of fiction to examine and probe, to reflect and promise. This is critical drama. The role playing, the improvisation, and the production of meaning can extend to any aspect of circumstance of the selected script. In this way the drama extends itself to the background of the students. Through this process students can use *The Flight of the Earls* to help them better understand their own circumstances. They can build on the play to fictionalize their own possibilities and can learn from the play that behind personal settings there are ideological and political forces at work. If these forces can be demystified then students can often overcome them. Students can also ask themselves to work on given circumstances and search out emancipatory moments not only in fiction but also in their own lives.

Hamlet

Hamlet is possibly the best known play in the English language. The title role is both the hope and bane of most actors. The actor has to work his way through the dramatic range of Hamlet. It is helpful to remember that Shakespeare's plays were written for the stage. The fact that a stage presentation of *Hamlet* is multidimensional and live, may not sit well with those who prefer to read Shakespeare. Reading rather than seeing may be something like listening to Monday Night Football with the television picture turned off. Certainly reading is not the way Shakespeare would want *Hamlet* to be experienced. This view is particularly ironic when dealing with Shakespeare's theatre where a multiplicity of levels and playing areas tell their own stories. Richard David (1978) suggests that Shakespeare would have welcomed the technical innovations of the modern stage. There is little doubt that the live actor is the most telling advantage stage has over reading.

> The presentation of the man Hamlet, with all his implications, by a great actor on a stage is a more direct, a more comprehensive, and a more striking communication than is to be received from the most sensitive reading of the text. (David 1978, 6)

In Shakespeare's tragedies the leading character is usually a person who arouses our sympathy and admiration. A recurring motif in serious drama is the imposition of some duty to be performed. The performance of this duty often leads to loss of reputation, love, or life (Brockett 1976). So it is with Hamlet. Told to take revenge on his father's murderer, Hamlet knows that his Uncle Claudius has murdered his father, married his mother, and claimed the throne of Denmark. This revenge means that Hamlet would become a murderer himself and possibly lose his own life. *Hamlet* is a gold mine for critical pedagogy because it contains so much raw material for questioning. It offers overt examples of power relationships, value systems, historical circumstances, and social commentary. On a more particular level, one of the great values of the role of Hamlet as a tool for critical analysis is the question of his sanity or his insanity. In fact Hamlet uses his insanity as a critical tool to interrogate the people and circumstances of the court. Students can make use of this scalpel of insanity to cut into other aspects of life in the house of Denmark. Working with their teachers, students could do some exploring with Hamlet and question him as he roams about the castle. Students could write or improvise a companion script that would allow them to interview servants or be present at royal meetings. These departures from Shakespeare's script would give students an opportunity to step outside the established fiction to make critical fiction of their own. Another useful critical device would be for students, in role as courtiers, to write a letter to a present-day classmate. This convention would enable students to examine the different culture of the writer and the receiver. A student could write a newspaper editorial about the significance of the insane activities going on in court. Whose sanity could students question? Another newspaper account could write about how the relations of social and governmental power, found in *Hamlet*, compare to the social and governmental settings in North America? Can students use the context of Royal Denmark to shed light on Ottawa, Washington, or London?

In a real sense *Hamlet* already has a critical companion script in *Rosencrantz and Guildenstern Are Dead* by Tom Stoppard (1967). This script is written outside the play about the Prince of Denmark and as such offers some unique insights into how existing dramatic fiction can be used for purposes of critical pedagogy. Rosencrantz and Guildenstern encounter Hamlet, as they do in Shakespeare's piece, but Stoppard now gives them a life of their own in his play. They are able to tell us things about the court of Denmark that we could never get from *Hamlet*. They, in a sense, become critical tools for our questions. Teachers, in struggling to invent a critical pedagogy, can certainly learn from Rosencrantz and Guildenstern.

One Flew Over the Cuckoo's Nest

One Flew Over the Cuckoo's Nest, written by Dale Wasserman (1974), is based on the novel by Ken Kesey. It is a difficult play to mount because it deals with the dramatically sensitive issue of mental illness coupled with brute physical and psychological force. However, it is the very coupling of the elements of sensitivity and brutality that gives this play its critical potential.

In a real sense *One Flew Over the Cuckoo's Nest* is itself a story about liberation. Patrick McMurphy is a tragic hero, not in the classical mode, but one who sacrifices himself so someone else can triumph. This play is as much about the repressive power of conformity as it is a documentation about life in an "insane asylum." The action for the play takes place in a hospital ward that is a sad and colorless place. Cheerless and hopeless patients who seldom smile or question inhabit the ward. Chief Bromden who has an ambivalent attitude to the whole place offers the narrative for this piece. In many ways *One Flew Over the Cuckoo's Nest* is Chief Bromden's story. Nurse Ratched, alias Big Nurse, represents the repression in the hospital. McMurphy swaggers into this house of repression and conformity. He looks, he questions, and he takes over. McMurphy fights the repression and conformity at every opportunity; and if there are no opportunities, he makes them. We can approach this play on many levels. At a minimal level it is an improbable cat and mouse game between the forces of confinement and escape. At another level the hospital ward is a metaphor for society. In a critical drama pedagogy the teacher and students can work at whatever level suits their educational needs.

One key critical question that we can address in *One Flew Over the Cuckoo's Nest* is the one of subjectivity. Students can examine the script of the play to see how the patients are viewed and treated. Is there a sense that these patients are mere objects of hospital care and cure? Some authority figure decides what is best for them. The patients have little or no say in their treatment. The administrators hold power over the patients and use it against them. McMurphy questions, challenges, and resists this authority. Because of this he becomes the enemy, and he must be silenced.

One of the critical values of this play is that the issues are not simple. First, there is the question of McMurphy's sanity. He might be certifiably psychotic. There is also a question of what is best for the patients. Does McMurphy know more about treating the patients that Nurse Ratched? On the surface it is a good guy against the bad institution. Is life—in *or* out of institutions—that simple? In fact we can see life as being very complex.

Is there any comparison, beyond a glib comment, between the institution examined in this play and the school that the teacher and students are working in? How do teachers and students use knowledge and power in the school, and for what purposes? Are students able to script or improvise a companion play that represents their experiences in school? This exercise should not be merely an invitation for students to compare negatively their school to the institution found in *One Flew Over the Cuckoo's Nest*. That could be too facile. If this play is used as a metaphor for students' lives, how can they suggest ways that indicate that they can become responsible for themselves? They could begin by seeing themselves in dramatic role, as patients on Nurse Ratched's ward. How could they respond? What could they do, even in small ways, to set themselves up as critical agents who have some measure of autonomy? What can they draw on from their own histories, experiences, and culture to sustain them under such conformity? How can these histories, experiences, and cultures be affirmed for and by the students in a way that empowers their real lives? How can the fiction influence reality?

It would also be of critical benefit to realize how students' reading of *One Flew Over the Cuckoo's Nest* differs from that of the teacher's. What activities would they see as repressive or a call for conformity? The teacher-in-role, as a Nurse Ratched or a Doctor Spivey, brings students to a point where they would no longer accept the repression and demands for conformity. The teacher-in-role as a McMurphy could tease out opportunities for students to resist the repression and conformity in their own way. These ways of resistance would not have to conform to the examples used by McMurphy in the original script. Part of the challenge, within a critical drama pedagogy, is to have students produce their own text. Students would need to realize that the patients in *One Flew Over the Cuckoo's Nest*, have potential that is not being realized. Even within the confines of an institution, people have possibilities that are beyond conformity. A language of possibility for such patients could revolve around being the most authentic, free, and independent person they could be within such constraints. Students need to realize that we all live within earth-bound constraints. It does not help social justice for a critical pedagogy to pretend that we need not live within constraints. Part of the challenge is to work the constraints in a way that transforms them.

Jesus Christ Superstar

Selecting a musical theatre piece to be part of a book on critical drama pedagogy might appear a bit tenuous. However, I am writing this book in light of the great variety of dramatic work that is reproduced and produced in schools. Some of this work involves musical theatre. Despite the blatant use of style and glitter, it is possible for some musical theatre to have critical moments. In many ways the musical is the Big Mac of drama; every taste you could possibly have the producers crowd into that one mammoth bun. Too often the basis for a musical is a sketchy plot that serves as an excuse for songs and chorus numbers. One of the remarkable things about musicals is that they are so popular. In many traditional musicals there is little connection with everyday life; rather there is a fascination with the romantic, faraway places, and unusual happenings.

One of the acritical ways that musical theatre works is to use music and design to lull the audience into tacit acceptance. Audiences seem to accept overt statements of feelings and intentions if presented in song. If similar statements were made in straight dialogue, the audience might be less comfortable. Musical theatre offers great scope for stage, lighting, and costume design. Very often such design simply means to look good, to dazzle. It is my contention that music and design can be used to give musical theatre critical moments. For purposes of exploring this claim, I will comment on the rock opera *Jesus Christ Superstar* (Andrew Lloyd Webber and Tim Rice (1973).

This musical drama has been used a lot in high schools. The story line deals with the last days of Jesus of Nazareth as he triumphs and is ultimately executed by the Romans. The story has many traits of a classic tragedy. The plot centers on a person who has become a popular figure who runs against the political wishes of Rome and the religious demands of Israel. These are powerful forces.

As with many musicals, it is possible to get lost in the driving rock music and special effects. However, there are many opportunities in this piece of theatre to examine social and political relationships. There are also openings to dissect the influences of religious and political ideologies on lived experiences. This musical theatre offers myriad interdependent social, historical, and political forms that the teacher and students can hold up against the students' own shared experience. Ultimately, *Jesus Christ Superstar* is about power relations. Students can examine the power relationships between the political forces under Pontius Pilate and the religious forces under Caiphas. They can investigate the class separations between the High Priests and the mob. With their teacher, students can inspect the personal relationships between Judas and Jesus, between Mary and Jesus, and between the Followers and Jesus. They can do all this while working with the script. There are also many critical opportunities for students while presenting the musical in public and while working outside the script.

Jesus Christ Superstar is one theatre piece that certainly can be played against itself. First, there is the element of using rock music over a religious story. There is an additional critical opening for making use of a traditional setting in contrast with the music form. In other words put Jesus and his contemporaries in historical garb while they communicate a universal story through rock songs. I believe this juxtaposition alone is enough to make us think. It is also possible to play the historical figures in different forms. For example, what critical questions are being asked, and openings being offered, if women play the High Priests' roles? This seems to me to be an ideal place to investigate the place of women in historical and patriarchal settings. We can do this educational work inside and outside the script. It is quite possible for students to produce their own text in relation to such a topic. The students, in collaboration with their teacher, could write or improvise scenes that would explore how a woman could get to be a high priest. What would have to be changed in historical times for that to happen? What do we need now for a woman to reach the relative position of a high priest? The educational value in such an exercise lies, in great part, in the quality of the dialectical reflection students are empowered to have. If these exercises lack reflection they will remain at the level of theatre games. Such games will contribute very little to a critical drama pedagogy.

While dealing with *Jesus Christ Superstar*, teachers must help students to explore and analyze the forces acting through and in their own lives. One of the important components of a critical pedagogy is to encourage students to realize that they too are often part of the forces they reflect on. The oppressed cannot be the only aim of a critical pedagogy. It must also seek the transformation of those who oppress. Very often, in subtle but insidious ways, we all oppress.

Jesus Christ Superstar gives us a great opportunity to examine the ideology that exists behind knowledge, politics, and power. This play has many vested groups fighting over the significance and threat of Jesus. Each group has its own political, religious, or cultural agenda: the Jews want to appease the Romans; the Romans want to dominate in peace; the High Priests do not want their religious authority challenged; and the people want a Messiah. Students can work inside the script to investigate the ideological motives that underpin specific utterances. The students, with help from their teacher, can work outside the script to produce text that will demystify the thinking of the religious, political, and community leaders. For example, there could be scenes that feature representatives from all groups as they debate from their own vested interests. The teacher could be in role as the convener of such a meeting where one powerful group can play against another. There also could be student-produced scenes, written or improvised, that would have members of a given group debating among themselves in relation to their own agenda.

In looking at a play like *Jesus Christ Superstar*, how can students realize the potential of their own society? How could the circumstances and power relations in this story change to transform the society of *Jesus Christ Superstar*? What could happen if the leaders of the various groups decided to cooperate? What would we need to get the political, religious, and community factions together in our society? Can we conceive of a situation where they would work toward a common goal? Can we not get beyond the disunited nations struggling in a broken promised land scenario?

I'm Not Rappaport

I'm Not Rappaport is a masterful play by Herb Gardner (1987). This play is about two octogenarians who are determined to live on without being put out to pasture. These two characters play off each other with telling wit and great resilience. One of the characters, Nat, is a lifelong radical who insists on fighting each new battle as if the revolution was in progress. He weaves stories and personalities out of his imagination to amuse and confuse those around him. Nat would never admit telling lies for he simply makes alterations to the truth. His park bench mate is Midge. Midge, an apartment superintendent, spends his days in Central Park. There he hides from his tenants who want him to retire.

In many ways this play is about growing old in North America. Nat sees himself as a pigeon in the park. He pretends that the food he requests is to feed the pigeons. It is not to feed the pigeons. Possibly Nat invents his stories and the necessary personas in order to fight off reality. His daughter worries about him and wishes to put him in a home for the aged. He fears that he will die there. This is not his image of old age. He relives the past and realizes that the ideas articulated at the time were better than the people that had them. In his old age he has become a man of hope. This is one of the positive openings for critical pedagogy.

Midge is being replaced because of automation. At least that is the surface story. In reality the tenants want him gone because of his age. Nat reminds the young that they collect old commodities but reject old people. These two people insist on fighting for their oldness. It is precious to them. Striving for dignity and independence, they are not willing to admit that the world belongs to the highest bidder. How can they hold on to their self worth in the face of ridicule and violence? Everyone wants to put them away. Nat reminds Midge that to remain honest we must cherish our enemies as we cherish our friends.

In the final analysis they refuse to give in. They refuse to give into their robbers, their tenants, their daughters, or to themselves. In the last scene, Nat tells Midge another story which represents the ongoing struggle for human dignity. Nat's stories transform their days. Each new story, told on that park bench, is a sign of hope.

How can teachers make use of *I'm Not Rappaport* to help students understand their own worlds? A play like this can serve our social investigation as a crack through which to question reality and suggest alternatives. Part of Nat and Midge's struggle is to have people respect them for the way they want to live out their lives. They certainly are not shy at articulating their world view. By working inside the script, students can examine the world view expressed by Nat and Midge. This examination can be helpful as a jumping-off point for a discussion on students' views of society and the place the elderly have in it. Students could debate the quality of a culture that has so little regard for the aged. It would be an interesting critical exercise to have students select certain dialogue from the two old gentlemen and play them as if they were thirty years of age. What factors change the meaning students would read from the same dialogue, when it is delivered by people who are not old? How would we react to the same statements? Would younger men make such statements? Could there be gender role reversals for this play? How would we react to two women making the same claims for dignity and independence? It would also be of critical interest to improvise or write a scene introducing characters who supported Nat and Midge in their quest for independence. How could such characters indicate this support? In what fashion would the affirmation of the old people be presented? Once again working outside the script, it would be critically useful to have students write themselves into the text. Have the young people meet the two gentlemen in the park. How would they treat them? Would the students even talk to them? Would there be any common points of interest? Here would be an opportunity for the students to work out their value system in relation to the place of the elderly in their society. What forces are working on the students to act in a certain way toward the elders? Would the students act differently if they were alone as opposed to being in a larger group? If they would act differently, why? The teacher could be in role as one of the old people. In this way the teacher could step out of the role for moments of the reflection that is such a critical part of the process. It is in the moments of reflection that the students really get to explore their own actions and value systems. It is in such moments that students are able to find their own voices and articulate what is important to them. It is in knowing their own lives that they are empowered. They then can make the adjustments that they see are necessary. This would have to be a free and nonevaluative process. There is no value in having the teacher tell the students how they should act toward the characters. This would not be critical pedagogy. The teacher can help the critical pedagogy process by aiding in the reflection. The teacher points to options, asks probing questions, and encourages dialogue. The teacher does not simply tell. The teacher facilitates student empowerment and ultimately student transformation.

The role playing and text production could continue as the students place themselves at the age of Nat and Midge. They could be other elderly people on other park benches. How would they differ from the two characters in *I'm Not Rappaport*? What in their biographies could help prepare them for such a life? What would they need to survive? Would it be possible for them to grow? How does their present life compare to the lived experience of these two men? This form of critical drama can help shape social consciousness.

SET AND LIGHTING DESIGN

The first level of a play that greets the participants and audience is design. However, in many ways design can imbue the play with a special logic of its own. Careful design can open up critical opportunities for the participants and audience to view the world of a play in a different light. The stage design should be expressive of a given play's artistic quality but can be much more than that. Design can give more than the mood, style, and theme of the play. It can be a tool for critical pedagogy.

Stage design uses the basic elements of line, shape, space, color, texture, and ornament. The mix and match of these elements are the openings not only for collective creativity but for critical design. These elements can be used against each other to create interest, dissonance, and signs of possibility.

In using the basic elements of design, it is possible to make use of certain principles to get artistic and critical effects. These principles of design are harmony, balance, proportion, emphasis, and rhythm. Mixing the basic elements of design, while using the guiding principles in a positive or negative fashion, can offer critical moments for a dramatic presentation or sharing. Using harmony, balance, proportion, emphasis, and rhythm and their opposites can be a powerful, critical tool.

Set and lighting design has become one of the crucial elements in professional and community theatre. The art of theatre is developing with the use of new materials and new possibilities offered by lighting. There is a drive by designers to use materials and techniques, invented for other purposes, in theatre. These material and technical developments can be seen aesthetically. In the history of staged drama, sets and lighting were often exclusively used to put the play in context and to give it enough light so the audience could see. Now theatre has the option of going beyond the utilitarian and allowing set and lighting to offer specific dramatic elements of their own. This change opens up real possibilities not only for theatre but for drama pedagogy as well. A set can build on the power of suggestion, for example, when a single element of a set is allowed to represent a full scene. If a set piece is used in this fashion, the audience can see through and behind the scene to allow the play to speak on two fronts; the front expressed by words and the front expressed by image. The background can be used to contradict what is said out front or reinforce some one aspect of the play that might lie dormant. In *Evita*, the Eva Peron character may be claiming "Don't cry for me, Argentina" while the see-through walls reveal the human devastation of the political reality. Designers should be free to use any material that serves their purpose. No longer is it necessary to be limited to wood and canvas. Designers should also be free to use styrofoam, wire netting, plastic, tubing, iron, plexiglass, rope, and cardboard. Designers should, I believe, look to the material surroundings of the people and culture involved in a play and use those. The very material used in making sets can be highly symbolic. For example, in a play about the homeless, what could be more telling than the use of cardboard boxes?

Set and lighting design is not given the same significance in school drama. There are many reasons for this. Often in school drama the entertainment of an audience is a secondary matter. The emphasis is more often on interpretation, characterization, confidence, and competency. Too often sets and lighting are seen as expensive and unnecessary. As far as critical drama pedagogy is concerned, the designs of sets and lighting are invaluable. One school of thought claims that sets and lighting should be used only to support the play. However, the images made possible through sets and lighting, offer great openings for inquiry and dissonance. Of course the use of sets and lighting will depend on the agenda for presenting a play. It is my contention that when drama is produced, the set and lighting have to be given the power of words. Images tell a story. Sets and lighting can be used to indicate the historical period, climate, socioeconomic conditions, cultural background, and governmental system. But sets and lighting can go beyond this type of revelation by playing against the script or overstating the contradictions inherent in the dramatic piece. Putting the patients from *One Flew Over the Cuckoo's Nest* in a wire cage, shouts the condition of confinement. The image of the patients clinging to that wire cage as they stare at the audience can be a very powerful one. It is very possible that this image is powerful beyond words. A set can also tell us much about the relationships of the various people in a play. In *Shirley Valentine*, the housewife can be confined to a tiny kitchen to emphasize how bound she is within her little life. This claustrophobic setting can be contrasted with the stage-wide expanse of her new life, lived out on a Greek beach. The message is in the contrast. In the kitchen, Shirley's husband rules by male decree. On the open beach, he shares her life by invitation. The kitchen is cold and the light is steel blue. The beach is warm and the light is golden amber. The set speaks.

One of the other opportunities in set and lighting design for critical pedagogy is to help the audience participants complete their own images. In other words the set pieces and lights hint at possibilities. *I'm Not Rappaport* calls for a massive bridge in the background. What if that bridge is not complete? Will not the audience members complete the bridge themselves as the play develops? Will greater power be given to that symbol if various actors try to use the uncompleted bridge? Why should we present audiences with completed bridges?

A set can help create an atmosphere. There might be critical value in putting an actor playing Hamlet, for example, in a setting that simply does not complement him. It is also possible to have the actor play the role against the setting: a gentle woman in a formal setting; a modern man in an archaic place. Play against the set. If the set for *Hamlet* consists of walls that are not at all perpendicular, then a big clue is given about "the state of Denmark." The dissonance between the order of the royal court and the staggered walls is evident. If the windows of this set are distorted in a way that invites the audience participants to view their own worlds differently, then a critical drama pedagogy can be at work. This use of set design is far beyond entertainment. This type of set demands inquiry and response. How do we straighten up the walls in our own homes and institutions? How do we distort the stories told and the parts played by our students? The questions go on.

Many different styles of set design are available for the drama teacher to build on (Ommanney and Schanker 1972). These various styles have value for critical drama pedagogy in so far as they can make a further inquiry and point to emancipatory possibilities.

Symbolism allows parts of the set to be used to make a central point about the play. For example, in *The Flight of the Earls* dominant, burned-out buildings can symbolize the destruction of a Northern Ireland community. Added to this, gradually collapsing walls in the down-stage setting of a farmhouse symbolize the internal collapse of the warring family. The whole set can be a metaphor for disintegration. How could critical drama students turn around these symbols and metaphors to indicate elements of integration and hope?

In the style of Expressionism we are talking about exaggerated symbolism that might be used to overstate a point. In *The Ecstasy of Rita Joe*, the magistrate might be seated on an oversized court bench to point out the dominance of a repressive and racist legal system. The magistrate sees all and is legal master of all he surveys. Before him Rita Joe is powerless. How can drama teachers help their students dismantle such an exaggerated symbol of power? How can students design a set that symbolically reverses the power relationships?

Impressionism, in set design, attempts to have the audience participants see through the character's eyes. In *Equus*, shiny metal heads are used to create the horse images in the minds of the protagonists. How can students, working through drama, build on this style to create images of personal and social possibility?

One of the most useful design styles for a critical drama pedagogy is Constructivism, which uses an architectural or mechanical skeleton to suggest a background for a play. Using this style, the drama teacher can help students design a background that symbolizes the social and economic circumstances that underpin a play. For example, in *Jesus Christ Superstar*, the massive skeletons of architectural pillars looming over the proceedings, can indicate the raw power wielded by the High Priest and Roman governor. These pillars can then serve as points of discussion and reflection for students and teacher.

I should note that there are other elements of drama that I have not emphasized. I am referring to the critical use of sound, costume, and make-up. The aural aspects of drama production could be most fruitful for critical pedagogy. In particular I am thinking about the ways sound can be used to play against dominant social messages. All these elements are crucial to a critical pedagogy of drama.

Critical drama must work against allowing the culture industry to use design for its own purpose. Design, as it can be used in critical drama, should have an emancipatory intent. One of the basic points I want to make here is that design style can be used to help students to think and judge for themselves. Design should not be used to hide the message and the context of a play. The intent here is not to simply captivate by design but to indicate and question. These processes can serve the cause of critical pedagogy.

6

Cultural Capital and Drama Processes

Rita: My uncle was Dan Joe . . . . He was dyin' and he said to me—long ago the white man comes with Bibles to talk to my people, who had the land. They talk for hundred years . . . then we had all the Bibles, an' the white man had our land.

George Ryga, *The Ecstasy of Rita Joe*

Part of the challenge in developing a critical pedagogy is not only to teach students about drama but to empower students through drama. This means we have to open up drama to the students. In a real sense teachers have to give students creative and reflective power over the drama processes, projects, and presentations. Cecily O'Neill writes, "A genuine encounter with theatre and an experience of learning can be a process of discovery and a process that can provide both a powerful sense of disclosure and illumination and a feeling of growing insight and mastery" (1991, 24).

That arts can give voice to students has been one of the chief claims made in this text. Students are able to connect their own experiences to drama and capitalize on their own culture. Those who bring their own culture to drama through drama can share that culture. Drama and culture are interdependent. The drama helps the culture. Students can hold out their own histories and experiences for the community to see. Then they can be more confident to go back to their stories and use them to produce drama, their own drama.

Drama is a social force, and teachers should use it as such. Most fine plays were not written on contract but were produced in a given culture to express some aspect of that culture. Students need the encouragement to do their own work. The teacher must provide openings for students to produce their own text. When teachers ask if students have something to say, the response is usually affirmative. As educators we may not always like what students say, but it is their voice. How can teachers structure (not in any restrictive sense) those voices to produce drama in a form that reflects and builds on students' voices? We do this, I think, by setting up an environment where students are free to speak. We can then take their comments and build reflection into them.

VOICE AS A PEDAGOGICAL CATEGORY

It is helpful for us to use the concept of voice as a pedagogical category to examine what possibilities drama has for students and teacher-learners. This exercise allows us to see what students bring to school as well as to realize the knowledge and culture students and teachers can produce between them. The world of knowledge can be brought home to students and teachers in their shared classrooms.

Knowledge and the production of knowledge can be made less external and more germane to the world of the students who must be able to express their understanding of the world. Teachers must realize that they can collaborate with their students to transform, where necessary, aspects of lived experiences. I see transformation working in an analogous fashion to hegemony. Transformation, which should be allowed to seep through our institutions and relationships usually comes in small doses and usually happens over time. Transformation usually happens with gentle hands. Transformation usually happens through cultural production.

Weiler (1988) put a lot of responsibility for this transformation in teachers' hands.

> Teachers are not simply parts of some mechanism of social reproduction; nor are their lives dictated by the demands of capital, racism, or patriarchy in such a way that they are automatons. Teachers are actors and agents in complex social sites where social forces powerfully shape the limits of what is possible. But these teachers retain the ability to be conscious and to analyze and act within this socially defined site. (1988, 148)

Student Voice

Giroux (1989) reminds us that language and lived experience are inseparable. For many reasons we speak out of our lived experience. In fact there might not be any other way to speak. Therefore, if we are not free to speak out of our experiences, we might not have any voice. If individual experience is negated, is it possible that the individual is negated? Silenced? Drama can be used to help students speak around these silences. In time, drama can help give voice to student experiences and therefore to students. Through drama, students can be given authorship. The stories of the students serve as the material for such authorship.

Once teachers help students realize that authors, accepted and published, write out of their own culture, students can see that such cultural production can be theirs also. Here students can find their voice. In drama the authorship can be in the form of improvisation, enactment, or script. Once students come to the realization that their authorship is liberating, they can build on that freedom.

Students can use this authorship to "reconstitute their relationship within the wider society" (Giroux 1989, 153). In a drama pedagogy, students are free to express and examine their own experiences in the light of other drama scripts. Better still, other drama scripts are examined in the light of students' experiences and their expressed culture. Students and teachers are able to step in and out of role in order to elucidate the circumstances and experiences of their own lives. The language used in drama can serve as a means to empower students to socially transform their lives. If students can develop a text for fiction, they might be able to produce a text that speaks to their own reality. This transformation is accomplished over time by building layers of confidence and self critique.

Drama, as a form of fiction, allows students and teacher-learners to speak their minds and share their circumstances in a relatively safe environment. In other words, students can speak the truth and call it fiction; they can disguise their worlds in fiction. Through this drama-fiction, teachers can likewise examine their own voices as they "actively produce, sustain, and legitimate meaning and experience in classrooms" (Giroux 1989, 159). As teachers work through drama, in and out of role, they maneuver between transmission and transformation. They can lay out the reality of drama content and skills as the raw material of transformation. The knowledge and skills of drama can be used as transformative tools for students to probe their own reality.

One of the hardest things for teachers to do is to share the process of learning with students. All our professional training and thinking is grounded in the assumption that we, as teachers, are supposed to know. It follows that we are supposed to tell. Unless we work against this instinct to tell, our teaching will remain limited. Yet, the teacher remains essential, and transmitting knowledge remains basic to learning. However, mere telling is not enough. As Cecily O'Neill wrote some time ago, "the function of the teacher is to challenge, arouse, interest, make anxious, give confidence, co-ordinate achievement, encourage reflection" (1976, 12). O'Neill wonders if drama teachers should not help students build new narratives rather than reenact the old narratives. If we can put emphasis on building rather than enacting, on producing rather than reproducing, then critical pedagogy is open to us. Skillful drama teachers will encourage students to ask their own questions which extend invitations to reflection. It is important that the teacher and student reflect together and make drama together. Drama is a most positive place for collaborative learning.

One of the difficulties with using art in schools, as I indicated earlier, is that it tends to be what the teacher makes it. In other words the teacher's background, interests, and attitudes often become the unintentional focus for a given drama program. Doubtless the cultural capital of the teacher will be a dominant factor in shaping a drama program in school. Still teachers have to remind themselves that is more important to be aware of the cultural capital of their students than it is to simply follow their own agenda. If the drama program is to serve the best interests of the students, it should reflect and build on their cultural capital. A teacher can, through in-role work, help students realize the authentic value of their different lifestyles, ethnic origins, or belief systems. All these differences can help make up the mosaic of a critical pedagogy.

Henry Giroux (1989), in a discussion on Mikhail Bakhtin and Paulo Freire, tells us that a critical pedagogy must begin with the concrete experiences of everyday life. It seems that school drama can be seen as a "cultural field where knowledge, language, and power intersect" (p. 133). This intersection can be a place where moral, cultural, and social practices are produced. One of the intentions of teachers working in school drama can be simply to give students voice. Sometimes the giving of voice is much more important than the presentation and the comprehension of new material. Teachers can simply give students a place to speak their part. This action gives new meaning to students having a part in a play. In this way, the part is theirs. Students are able to use their experiences, their cultures, and their stories. This in itself is a real form of power for students. Out of these parts, new confidences grow, new social relationships are put in place, and new meanings can be produced.

Another aspect of critical pedagogy is the absolute need for teachers to know their students, who just have to mean more to teachers than seating arrangements, completed assignments, and test scores. Teachers, working through critical drama, must be "attentive to the histories, dreams, and experiences that students bring to school" (p. 142). Giroux also cautions that such student parts should not only be affirmed but examined for their personal, cultural, and political significance.

An agenda that authentically calls for student voices, it should be noted, demands a classroom setting that allows such sharing and dialogue. In particular, students must physically face each other. The form of the classroom speaks to the quality of the process. Schools are not like the old churches where the very structure of the place demands silence from the many. Expecting students to tell their stories, play their parts, to the backs of fellow students' heads is patently ridiculous.

Teacher Voice

Yet another significant factor in critical drama is the teacher's voice, which I believe is the single greatest tool in developing a critical pedagogy. The teacher is a gatekeeper between the dominant culture of the school and the individual student. The drama teacher must learn to use the language of drama to free rather than confuse. The language and skills of drama, and theatre in particular, can be very mystifying. This language and these skills can also serve as gate openers. Teachers can use their own stories, their own parts, to foster a critical pedagogy of drama. We should, I believe, tell students our stories; but they must be true stories. We cannot bring our stories with crooked hands. Our stories, our parts, must not simply be devices to instruct, or to draw out student stories. We must not present our authentic stories in an acritical fashion. If teachers approach their own knowledge and experience in a critical fashion, the message will not be lost on students. Teachers must be able to stand back from their own stories. Affirmation and critique go hand in hand. How can we expect students to value each other's stories if ours are seen as hidden. A critical pedagogy of drama calls for collaboration. We learn from student stories and teacher stories. We cannot simply ask the students to collaborate on their own. Teachers have to be part of that collaboration. As Joyce Edwards and Therese Craig (1990) noted in their research, the more input students have with the ideas of drama, the greater their engagement in the process. Ownership of ideas is an important empowerment in a critical drama pedagogy.

One of the greatest ways for drama teachers to give voice to their students is through the convention of teacher-in-role. John Carey (1990) believes that if teachers free themselves enough to take on a role in drama, a significant change can be made in the balance of power in the classroom. Working in role requires a great deal of trust between students and teachers. Using a teacher-in-role strategy still calls for the teacher to make demands and establish responsibilities. The teacher must still function as enabler, still be responsible for the class. One of the great disservices done to transformative education is the notion that the students do what they like. Of course, use of this phrase has strong hegemonic significance. A teacher can work in role, be enabling and responsible, and still be collaborative. The need here is for the teacher to work inside the drama. The teacher negotiates rather than dictates the drama. One of the other important messages here is that the teacher is learning with the students. If working in role helps remove the authoritative and judgmental elements often found in drama, then another link can be fashioned in a network of critical pedagogy.

> I would like to suggest that by working in role we, as teachers, are able to establish a pattern of relationships which enable negotiation, joint ownership and the sharing of power even if elsewhere the normative role of the teacher is a traditional one. And furthermore that the fictional interaction provides a model for the real classroom interaction that students are able eventually to adopt. (Carey 1990, 7)

One of the helpful distinctions Stuart Bennett (1984) makes in relationship to teacher role is to suggest that teachers can control the quality of the learning rather than controlling the content. The objective is to enable students and teachers to construct real meanings for themselves. In order to do this, students need to get behind the real significance of the events that constitute the material of the drama. Teachers do not have to present themselves as having the answers to problematic situations; rather, they are involved with the students in finding a solution: "Society maintains an equilibrium of conventional wisdom. If you ask questions of this wisdom it appears to consider changing its position but in fact does not. It is a constantly readjusting equilibrium" (p. 23).

If we begin drama with the understanding that people make their own culture, then we can more easily allow that drama to be critical. If we begin with trying to tap into the culture of the students rather than with some received culture, then critical pedagogy is already in place. It is important for us to remember that culture is a lived experience, one that is ever changing (Rose 1991). If we as teachers are dealing with student culture, then the drama is an extension of that culture. In its simplest form, this is critical pedagogy of drama at work. Through this drama, students can work toward self-empowerment and social transformation. Here particular forms of social knowledge and power relationships can be divested of their oppressive trappings. Students can build on their experiences in drama, based on the cultural material of their own lives, to question, resist, and transform the larger society. Institutional and social transformation is, I believe, achieved in small steps with the assistance of critical attitudes. Here lie the possibilities of emancipation.

REFLECTION

Reflection is one of the key ingredients in critical pedagogy. This reflection has several implications for drama teachers. First, it is essential for the students and their teacher to leave time for reflection about the drama experience. The teacher must make opportunities for reflection which can be done during or after the drama experience. Second, I would suggest that reflection be built into the drama. This is where teacher student dialogue comes in. If any drama experience is treated in a dialectical fashion, then questions will naturally follow. Through reflection students and teachers can learn to examine the relationships between power and knowledge in a fashion that sheds light on the production of such knowledge (Schon 1983, 1987). In this way they make use of the concept of teaching and learning as a process of inquiry into the problematic.

Dorothy Heathcote (1980) claims that the end product of drama is changed students. If drama is to do this, it has to operate in a critical fashion in the public world. For too long drama has had "doing" as its first priority. This may reflect an anti-intellectual attitude as much as a selected methodology. However, beyond doing and feeling there must be reflective thinking. This reflection must be connected to biography, history, culture, and politics. David Hornbrook (1989) states that theoreticians of drama have built their conceptual home in a general philosophy that denies politics and culture. Critical pedagogy can move to change this general philosophy.

A critical pedagogy of drama must invite students and teachers to give text to their own work. I am being careful here not to limit the production of new drama to script writing. I want to include the dramatic forms of role playing and improvisation. This production can be a form of living drama. Of course there can be a combination of role playing, improvisation, and script. Students can be given models from which to build their own drama in the context of a critical pedagogy.

Students have all kinds of stories to dramatize. Dramatic raw material lies at their finger tips for their lives are the very stuff of drama. Their lives are teeming with frustrations and hopes, their days are filled with resistance and encouragement, and their nights are flush with wandering and awe. Because students have the stories, teachers must give them the scope to work out those stories. Students and teachers can share themes of hardship and adventure, of confinement and pride. They can hear family accounts and build telling drama around these accounts. They can fictionalize their dreams and find a voice for such dreams through drama. The world of drama is filled with examples of such work.

EXAMPLES OF CRITICAL MODELS

In this section of the text I want to look at some examples of drama, that in a very real sense, serve as critical models. Among these examples, I plan to sprinkle suggestions for teachers and students who wish to use drama in this critical fashion.

First of all, I want to mention the work of Athol Fugard, who is regarded as South Africa's premier playwright and an ardent foe of that country's racist policies. I have chosen Fugard here because his plays celebrate an undying belief in human quality and equality. He also writes in the hope that justice will prevail; he struggles for that justice through his plays. Fugard (1991) claims that when he discovered what he wanted to talk about he found his voice. This is something teachers should remember about their students. When students are helped to discover their authentic selves, they will discover their voices. That is what Jamie Paul, in *The Ecstasy of Rita Joe*, is talking about when he asks to be told about himself so that he can get his voice back and be a whole person again.

In a very real sense Fugard has helped give theatre a place to voice the ills of South African apartheid. Even in the face of political reform, his work remains a challenge to world thinking about South Africa. He brings tremendous eloquence and humanity to his work. His many plays include *The Blood Knot*, *Hello and Goodbye*, *Sizwe Bansi Is Dead*, *The Island*, *A Lesson from Aloes*, *Master Harold . . . and the Boys*, and *My Children! My Africa!* These plays continue the critical educational process attained by Fugard, who is quite aware of the way that his work is regarded.

> There's a great danger when you move into an area of social concern, when social issues become part of the fabric of your story, you can become overly didactic, overly polemical in saying things. I suppose what has helped me avoid the worst excesses in that direction is . . . I'm a storyteller who is passionately interested in people. I always keep the human element in the forefront because I've always got a story about

a specific individual in mind, not a political idea. (Fugard 1991, 16)

Fugard sees himself primarily as a storyteller. This claim, of course, does not prevent his plays from being political. Fugard says he does not have to go looking for his plays, they come to him. His plays demand to be written.

Students, working in collaboration with their teachers, can also produce plays that can help them explore the forces that are acting on their lives. The forces acting on their lives do not always have to be as tragic as those in Fugard's homeland. The forces are real but not necessarily malevolent. Students, like Fugard, will write what is important to them. They will look around them and see what is important to them. They will be moved by a friend's sickness, devastated by a friend's suicide, made well by a loving word, saddened by a lost love. Students will turn their heads away from the images of starving children. They will rally as the walls are torn down, celebrate with their teams, and find hope in their futures. And, with encouragement and a safe environment, they will produce drama about these things. They will tell their own stories and reflect on their own lives. Because of this work they might see themselves differently. They just might change the society they live in. Students, too, can learn that if we do not offer solutions we will perpetuate the problems.

What other drama can we show students to indicate it as a transformative medium? Who else would need to use drama to examine their lives and the forces that drive such lives? Of course, there are many groups that turn to drama in order to express and examine their lives.

One such expression can be found in the native theatre of the Americas. In many ways Native American people are creating new theatre. Emerging as a theatre that is fresh and vibrant, it is not simply an appropriation of the white European culture. There is a felt need in native communities to transcend creating work that is simply a reaction to dominant culture. Native theatre artists no longer want to be the other. They wish to reclaim the power of the word and tell their own stories, for themselves, in their own way. However, native artists realize that with such self-definition comes responsibility.

In reclaiming the power of the word, they need not write and perform in the ancient languages of the first nations. It is possible for such writing and such performance to be done in English, French, or any imported language. It is possible to synthesize the language of colonization into a new theatrical language used as a transformative tool. This synthesis itself is helpful as it symbolizes a type of coexistence between languages and worlds; and by inference, between people.

> It is significant that the healers as artists are in the vanguard of this critical time. We are fertile minds from a living culture-ancient as well as contemporary. We are caught up on a wave of the cycle where, in our own words, we can approach the preservation, recognition, and continuation of our cultures, with decolonized minds. (Mojica 1991, 3)

Students need to be able to examine how they fit into the wider formation of society. If they are to transform themselves, within that society, they will need to be able to look at themselves under a new spotlight: drama. The students too will be able to "reclaim the power of the word" for themselves. They will be able to tell their own stories for they have lives of their own, their own culture. Their culture is more than a part of the larger culture, more than a reaction to a dominant adult culture. Students have their own language, symbols, and metaphors. These can be used in a new theatrical communication that can be transformative in that it can legitimize students' own voices and give them the tools to explore and analyze the forces acting on their own lives. When they know the forces acting on their lives, they will be able to grapple with such forces if they wish. Then they can give subjectivity and experience a stronger stance within their school lives. They will, with their teacher's help, be able to distinguish between the drama they reproduce and the drama they may produce. There is a world of difference between the two processes.

When students write or improvise their own stories, in a drama form, they are in a position to affirm the best dimensions of their own histories, experiences, and culture. They will be able to synthesize their language with the language of the school and community culture. This, in itself, is empowering. There is a chance for students to bring their own cultural capital to the foreground. If this is done, drama can point to the possibilities embedded in students' cultural traditions. Drama used in this way can help develop autonomous, independent, and critical individuals.

Playwright Tomson Highway writes about the myths and taboos of contemporary society. He wishes us to look deeply "into the waters and fires of our own experience, sensation and memory. Part of his project . . . is to aid in the decolonization of our minds and relationships through critical reflection" (Loveks 1991, 11). Highway has chosen to explore the sites of contest and decolonization through plays that deal with spirituality, nature, and gender. Seeing these aspects intertwined as one, he believes that there should be a sacred relationship between land, women, men, and children. In his plays Highway reveals that there is now a disconnection and a distortion of such a sacred principle and asks us to take a second look at ourselves. Highway challenges the taken-for-grantedness of our daily lives as he seeks out honesty, sharing, and contradiction. Critical drama can build on this approach.

If educators look to the words honesty, sharing, and contradiction, we can learn a lot about approaching a critical pedagogy. As educators we could remind ourselves that critical pedagogy has to do with self-empowerment and social transformation. This is a formidable agenda but one we must take seriously if we are to help students be more than fodder for industry and state. In approaching the world of the students, we must approach it honestly. Only then can we help them make a real difference. We have to respect how they see their world. How could teachers presume to be in a better position to understand the students' world than the students themselves? Yet we operate as if we know. We need to step back from our all-knowing stance as if we could give students self-empowerment. Yet, with a constructive attitude and critical skills we can help students gain self-empowerment. When students tell us something through drama we must be willing to listen to them. We ought to use their understandings to probe and to affirm possibilities in a safe pedagogical environment.

A word of caution is appropriate here. If students are to tell their stories they must not be held up to ridicule or derision. When students tell about the conditions of their childhood, this telling must be taken seriously. This is a crucial place for teachers to be aware of the cultural capital of their students. Teachers, by being sensitive to these stories, can give a voice to students who normally would not speak either for themselves or their families. It is here that a teacher can help students realize the authentic value of different lifestyles and value systems. If the classroom is a safe haven, the students will be able to discuss their circumstances with each other. Students live in a teasing, pointing, joking world that wounds many. Teachers can learn to cut through these barbs and even capitalize on them. In fact teachers can incorporate the negative comments into the drama. The nature of the barbs can be examined for their positive moments. Frequently the words we use don't always represent what we mean to say. So much of our dialogue is reaction. Students and teachers should set themselves free to decode such reactions.

One of the elements of critical drama that I have not emphasized is the factor of teacher voice. Teachers are constantly talking without having a voice. A speaker only has voice if that person is listened to. Honesty can be a very powerful tool for a critical educator. Part of the on-going challenge in teaching is to be authentic; however it is not always easy to be real for our students. To be transformative though, we have to be real because so much of our work is based on dialogue. It is very hard to have a sharing dialogue if we are not authentic. When we listen to students' histories and experiences we can learn about ourselves as well as about them. We can learn to be self-reflective and try to understand our own thinking and assumptions. This is especially true when our thinking and assumptions can have an impact on students. We cannot take our own thinking patterns for granted.

Teachers need to realize also that student opposition is an important activity. Student opposition can be a form of seeking for voice. The opposition we see from students is a part of their lived culture; and in many ways, it is an expression of that culture. Sometimes we give negative attention to such resistance. Certainly teachers do not have to accept every act of resistance executed by students. Some outbursts of resistance are no more than disruptive. If the resistance is not counter hegemonic, then it might be unacceptable. There is a dialectical relationship between learning and teaching and part of this relationship has to do with appreciating the role of resistance in education. As educators we must realize that student resistance in schools is part of a political struggle for power. That students seek power is not necessarily a negative factor in schooling. If we cannot accept the resistance aspects of student activity, then we may not be able to view students as critical agents or have real dialogue with them. In such a case we will be simply trying to win them over to our way of thinking. In this way we might be unable to make the knowledge we deal with meaningful to our students who will simply go on treating it as teachers' knowledge. If such knowledge is not theirs, it cannot be used for emancipatory moments or for social transformation. It is important for us to realize that we cannot change schools without student help. This means that we cannot change schools without giving students power. It follows from this that students cannot be empowered unless teachers are empowered (Aronowitz and Giroux 1985). The critical and honest dialogue that teachers need must be with students as well as with other teachers. What can students learn from playwrights like Tomson Highway? How can his emphasis on spirituality, nature, and gender lead us to a drama that is emancipatory? How can teachers help their students see that spirituality, nature, and gender are intertwined? How can teachers help students realize that they do live in a cultural realm built around spirituality, nature, and gender? Many students, teachers are correct in claiming, would deny that a student's life has anything to do with nature or the spiritual. In many cases students might be simply using other words for spiritual or natural. However, adults can learn from teenagers a lot about caring, which I am inclined to put in the realm of the natural and spiritual. Students, in general, are more free with gender issues than we are. Their rituals are built more around friends than around gender groups. This tendency is a useful opening for critical drama. If we watch students dance, we realize that they are more caught up with the dancing than with the gender of the dancing partner. In this way they are quite able to demonstrate, in drama, the forces that move them. They are able to move slowly to the memory of a lost friend. They are able to point a tormenting finger at the force that caused the grief. They are able to repair a broken promise. In short, they are able to be there, that is to keep the greatest existential promise of all.

Highway wants us to see the disconnection and distortion in our lives. He would have us work toward healing the disconnections and smoothing out the distortions. Students may wish to produce drama that would deal with the disconnections and distortions caused by unemployment, homelessness, or abuse. Students often do not have to go outside their own communities for dramatic raw material. Their drama may also demonstrate the dignity of work given, of a home shared, or of an abuse prevented. Students and their teachers can learn to share their knowledge through drama to interrogate the contradictions of our worlds. In sharing and honesty the contradictions of society will be seen in a clearer light where the contradictions can be used to open new possibilities. The disconnections and distortions need not be permanent.

I want to continue using Indian plays to search for elements that students can use in the production of their own drama. Hanay Geiogamah (1991) claims that in recent decades Native Americans have begun to realize that show dancing and historical pageants, designed for non-Indians, are not the only elements that could be used to build a native theatre. Over time realistic plays written by Indians for Indian audiences began to emerge. Through these plays

Indians found a new respect for ritual and form. This drama helped Native Americans define their own identities and succeeded because it offered an accurate reflection of contemporary Indian life. This drama is also a weapon against the hostility, ignorance, and insensitivity shown in film and on television.

Margo Kane (1991) reminds us of the need to uncover the stories buried within us and give voice to the characters within us. Kane uses her central character as a way to travel, as a means to journey. This storytelling, which does not have to be script bound, can change with each telling and can be a freeing form for critical pedagogy to use. It also might be an opportunity for us to think more in terms of recovering rather than reproducing a culture.

BEYOND ARTISTIC PERFORMANCE

As I have indicated earlier, student culture is filled with ritual and form. Such rituals and form often go unnoticed by students. They, like adults, take much for granted. It might be of interest for students to try to unravel some of the rituals that permeate their culture. For example, why do they travel in such large groups? Is there some tribal instinct at work here? If so, we should be very hesitant to break that ritual down. The reason for such groupings could be examined in drama. Within such grouping there are roles and pecking orders. How do students set these roles and pecking orders? What is affirmed in student groups that allow for the establishment of roles and pecking orders? Do these roles and pecking orders reflect something similar in the larger society? Or do they reflect values and behavior in opposition to the dominant culture? These are not only academic questions, they are valuable questions for students to ask. Students can produce their own drama to study these situations. If students were to start their own community, how would they live? What lifestyles would they advocate? What laws would they want established? Would group rights come before individual rights? How would they want their values passed on? Would they have sites for instructional reasons? Would there be leaders? What forms would leadership take? This drama project could be done over time with students and teacher building their own fictional community. In the reflective parts of this long-term drama project, students could ponder the possibility of bringing some of their fiction to the real world. What would they want to bring with them? What conditions would need to change before the students' ideal community could function?

Drama can also be used to help students define their own identities. Students spend much of their time caught between the worlds of childhood and adulthood. This is not always an easy place to be. Students can use drama to help them realize that their world has authentic boundaries of its own. Certain qualities of thought and feeling in a student's life give that life legitimacy. Student life is more than a limited version of adult life. In critical drama, students need to be able to act out freely their particular responses to life's circumstances. If students are dramatizing their reality, there must be opportunities to reflect on and analyze that reality. Here is an opportunity for teachers to give subjectivity and student experience a stronger stance in the whole process of schooling. If students are free to tell their view of the school and their place in it, then it is possible that school faculty will listen. I believe that student drama should get beyond the presentation of skits that merely entertain. However, there can be in these small dramatic presentations moments of resistance that can indict as well as show possibilities. Student-produced drama affords a unique opportunity to look at the structures and relationships that pervade schooling. How do teachers treat students? What levels of cooperation are evident among teachers? Do administrators see teachers as their workers or as their colleagues? Do students treat disadvantaged students with the respect they deserve? What negative aspects of the school are students trying to change? How can they carry these attempts to the larger community? In short, where does the transformation begin?

Students, in collaboration with their teachers, can use drama to give an accurate reflection of contemporary life. In some ways students are in a good position to stand back from society for they do not necessarily have the vested interests of adult stakeholders.

In this, they are free to probe the larger society. They are in a safe place. They can point to the examples of hostility, ignorance, and insensitivity that saturate our society. They can also dramatize that a handshake can curb hostility, that a knowing word can soften ignorance, and that a firm rebuke can temper insensitivity. All this can be done in dramatic form after good critical reflection.

CONCLUSION

One of the values in using drama as a form of critical pedagogy is to permit students "to examine the underlying political, social, and economic foundations of the larger society" (McLaren 1989, 169). In drama, students can be given the opportunity to examine the real significance of their shared knowledge. Students are given occasions to sift their knowledge for the ingredients of status, power, and privilege that contaminate it. In drama, students analyze culture, their own and others', in order to realize that such cultures are not simply deposited but are produced. When students appreciate that culture can be produced, through drama and other means, they can also see the power they have. This power is beyond artistic performance.

Drama, when used in a critical form, represents a site where students can inquire into the literary forms that are presented through the school curriculum. The students can see, through drama experiences that given curriculum forms affirm and disaffirm certain individuals and groups. This inquiry begins with accepted drama scripts and extends to the collaborative scripts. Whether the scripts are written or unwritten, the plays are produced by students. Students begin to understand that the plots, characters, and circumstances of scripted material are not neutral. Any scripted material carries the weight of the particular culture in which it was produced. This process goes far beyond performance.

In drama, teachers are able to step outside their authority roles and into roles of productive fiction. Through the rituals of drama, teachers may be able to see how their choice of plays, group arrangements, class management techniques, and instructional styles give unintended lessons to their students. Teachers can further help their students to become critically literate in so far as the drama group works at breaking down the ideological underpinnings of selected and produced plays. If students can decode scripted and produced plays, they can be more critical of the world beyond plays. They can be positive contributers to the process of meaning-making. Students can, with the help of enabling teachers, examine how the powers at work in plays are also at work in their lives. A critical eye is a first step toward self-empowerment and social transformation. We need to help our students look at the world in a new way. They need to see that they have power over their own lives and seek power over the community around them. In this way students and teachers, both individually and collectively, can actively advocate transformation.

Bibliography

Adorno, Theodor. "Culture Industry Reconsidered." *New German Critique* (Fall 1975): 12–19.

————. *Aesthetic Theory*. London: Routledge & Kegan Paul, 1984.

Adorno, Theodor, and Max Horkheimer. *Dialectic of the Enlightenment*. New York: Herder & Herder, 1972.

Akins, William. "Child Drama in University." *Theatre News* (Dec. 1981): 1–9.

Allen, John. *Drama in Schools: Its Theory and Practice*. London: Heinemann Educational Books, 1979.

Apple, Michael. *Ideology and Curriculum*. London: Routledge & Kegan Paul, 1979.

————. *Education and Power*. Boston: Ark Paperbacks, 1985.

Aronowitz, Stanley, and Henry Giroux. *Education Under Siege*. South Hadley: Bergin & Garvey Publishers, 1985.

Bates, Richard J. "Educational Critique, the New Sociology of Education, and the Work of Teachers." *Journal of Education* 163, no. 4 (Fall 1981): 306–19.

Belsey, Catherine. *Critical Practice*. London: Routledge, 1980.

Bennett, Stuart. *Drama: The Practice of Freedom*. London: National Association for the Teaching of Drama, 1984.

Bennett, Tony. *Popular Culture: History and Theory*. London: Open University Press, 1981.

Beyer, Landon E. "Ideology and Aesthetic Education." *American Educational Research Association* (1980): 39–41.

————. "Aesthetic Experience for Teacher Preparation and Social Change." *Educational Theory* 35, no. 4 (1985): 385–97.

Boal, Augusto. *Theater of the Oppressed.* London: Pluto Press, 1979.

Bolton, Gavin. *Towards a Theory of Drama in Education.* New York: Longman, 1979.

————. *Drama as Education.* New York: Longman, 1984.

Bourdieu, Pierre. *Outline of a Theory of Practice.* Cambridge: Cambridge University Press, 1977.

Bourdieu, Pierre, and Jean-Claude Passeron. *Reproduction in Education Society and Culture.* London: Sage Press, 1977.

Brockett, Oscar. *The Essential Theatre.* New York: Holt, Rinehart and Winston, 1976.

Brown, Firman. "The Rededication of the Great Profession of Teaching." *Design for Arts in Education* 14 (1991): 13–15.

Carey, John. "Teaching in Role and Classroom Power." *Drama Broadsheet* 7 (Summer 1990): 2–7.

Carnegie Forum on Education and the Economy. Task Force on Teaching as a Profession. *A Nation Prepared: Teachers for the 21st Century.* Washington, D.C.: The Forum, 1986.

Connelly, M., and Clandinin, D. *Teachers as Curriculum Planners.* Toronto: OISE Press, 1988.

Courtney, Richard. *Play, Drama and Thought: The Intellectual Background to Drama in Education.* New York: Drama Book Specialist, 1974.

————. *The Rarest Dream.* London: NATD, 1984.

David, Richard. *Shakespeare in the Theatre.* Cambridge: Cambridge University Press, 1978.

Davis, D., and C. Lawrence, eds. *Gavin Bolton: Selected Writings.* New York: Longman, 1986.

Dewey, John. *Art as Experience.* New York: Perigree Books, 1934.

Doyle, Clar. *A Site for Critical Pedagogy.* St. John's, Newfoundland: Memorial University of Newfoundland, 1989.

————. "A Foundation for Critical Aesthetic Education." In Amarjit Singh and Ishmael J. Baksh (eds.) *Dimensions of Newfoundland Society and Education.* vol. 1, 323–29. St. John's: Memorial University of Newfoundland, 1991.

Edwards, Joyce, and Therese Craig. "A Teacher Experiments with Drama as a Teaching Tool." *The Alberta Journal of Educational Research* 36, no. 4 (Dec. 1990): 337–51.

Eisner, Elliot. *The Educational Imagination.* New York: Macmillian Publishing Co., 1979.

Esslin, Martin. *The Anatomy of Drama.* London: Abacus, 1978.

Foucoult, Michel. *Power/Knowledge.* New York: Pantheon Books, 1980.

Freire, Paulo. *Pedagogy of the Oppressed.* New York: Continuum, 1981.

————. *The Politics of Education.* South Hadley, MA: Bergin & Garvey, 1985.

Fugard, Athol. *Dramatics* (September 1991): 14–20.

Gardner, Herb. *I'm Not Rappaport.* New York: Samuel French, 1987.

Geiogamah, Hanay. "Indian Theatre in the United States." *Canadian Theatre Review* (Fall 1991): 12–14.

Gibson, Rex. *Critical Theory and Education.* London: Hodder and Stoughton, 1986.

Giroux, Henry A. *Ideology, Culture and the Process of Schooling.* Philadelphia: Temple University Press, 1981.

————. "Culture and Rationality in Frankfurt School Thought: Ideological Foundations for a Theory of Social Education." *Theory and Research in Social Education* 9, no. 4 (Winter 1982): 17–55.

————. *Theory and Resistance in Education.* London: Heineman Educational Books, 1983.

————. "Marxism and Schooling: The Limits of Radical Discourse." *Educational Theory* 34, no. 2 (Spring 1984): 113–35.

————. "Literacy and the Pedagogy of Voice and Political Empowerment." *Educational Theory* 38, no. 1 (Winter 1988): 61–75.

————. *Schooling for Democracy.* London: Routledge, 1989.

————, ed. *Postmodernism, Feminism, and Cultural Politics.* Albany: State University of New York Press, 1991.

Goldman, Emma. *The Social Significance of Modern Drama.* New York: Applause Theatre Book Publishers, 1987.

Golsberg, Moses. *Children's Theatre: A Philosophy and a Method.* Englewood Cliffs, NJ: Prentice-Hall, 1974.

Greene, Maxine. *Landscapes of Learning.* New York: Teachers College Press, 1978.

————. "Breaking Through the Ordinary: The Arts and Future Possibility." *Journal of Education* 162, no. 3 (Summer 1980): 8–26.

————. *The Dialectic of Freedom.* New York: Teachers College Press, 1990.

Grumet, Madeline. "In Search of Theatre: Ritual, Confrontation and the Suspense of Form." *Journal of Education* 162 (Winter 1980): 93–110.

Hamblen, Karen A. "Approaches to Aesthetics in Art Education: A Critical Theory Perspective." *Journal of Issues and Research in Art Education* 29, no. 2 (Winter 1988): 81–90.

Haseman, Brad. "Improvisation: Process Drama and Dramatic Art." *The Drama Magazine* (July 1991): 19–21.

Hawksley, Fred. "Drama Education: Rehearsing for the Future." In Amarjit Singh and Ishmael J. Baksh. *Dimensions of Newfoundland Society and Education.* vol. 1, 330–37. St. John's: Memorial University of Newfoundland, 1991.

Heaney, Seamus. *The Haw Lantern.* London: Faber and Faber, 1987.

Heathcote, Dorothy. *Drama as Context.* Aberdeen: Aberdeen University Press, 1980.

Held, David. *Introduction to Critical Theory.* Los Angeles: University of California Press, 1980.

Holmes Group. *Tomorrow's Teachers: A Report of the Holmes Group.* East Lansing, MI: Holmes Group, 1986.

Hopkins, David. "The Role of the Practicum in Bridging the Gap between School and University." Paper presented to the Conference of the Western Canadian Association for Student Teaching. Edmonton, Alberta, Canada, March 13, 1980.

Hornbrook, David. *Education and Dramatic Art.* Oxford: Blackwell, 1989.

————. "Towards a Theory." *Drama Broadsheet* 7 (Spring 1990): 6–8.

Humble, Christopher. *The Flight of the Earls.* New York: Samuel French, 1984.

Jackson, Tony, ed. *Learning through Theatre.* Manchester: Manchester University Press, 1980.

Jagerman, Helen. *Directions in Drama Education: A Progress Report.* ERIC1987. ED 290 172.

Jay, Martin. *The Dialectical Imagination.* Boston: Little, Brown and Co., 1973.

Juliebo, Moira, Judith Thiessen, and Bruce Bain. "Drama: The Perfect Lure." *The Drama Magazine* (March 1991): 7–9.

Kane, Margo. "From the Centre of the Circle the Story Emerges." *Canadian Theatre Review* 68 (Fall 1991): 26–29.

Kempinski, Tom. *Duet for One*. London: Samuel French, 1981.

Kirk, David. "Beyond the Limits of Theoretical Discourse in Teacher Education: Towards a Critical Pedagogy." *Teaching and Teacher Education* 2, no. 2 (1986): 155–67.

Livingstone, David, ed. *Pedagogy and Cultural Power*. South Hadley, MA: Bergin & Garvey, 1987.

Loveks, Bryan. "Another Glimpse: Excerpts from a Conversation with Tomson Highway." *Canadian Theatre Review* 68 (Fall 1991): 9–11.

Male, Corinne. "Education and Dramatic Art: A Classroom Teacher's Perspective." *2D* 9, no. 2 (Summer 1990): 5–17.

Marcuse, Herbert. *Negations*. Boston: Beacon Press, 1968.

———. *An Essay on Liberation*. Boston: Beacon Press, 1969.

———. *The Aesthetic Dimension*. Boston: Beacon Press, 1978.

Martin, Wilfred. *Student Views on Schooling in Newfoundland and Labrador*. St. John's: Memorial University of Newfoundland, 1985.

McCann, Philip. "Culture, State Formation and the Invention of Tradition: Newfoundland." *Journal of Canadian Studies* 23 (Spring/Summer 1988): 86–103.

McCaslin, Nellie. *Creative Drama in the Classroom*. New York: Longman, 1980.

———, ed. *Children and Drama*. New York: Longman, 1981.

McLaren, Peter. *Life in Schools*. White Plains: Longman, 1989.

McLellan, David. *Marxism after Marx*. Boston: Houghton Mifflin Co., 1979.

McNeil, Linda. *Contradictions of Control*. New York: Routledge & Kegan Paul, 1986.

McSweeney, Maxine. *Creative Children's Theatre*. South Brunswick: A. S. Barnes, 1974.

Medoff, Mark. *Children of a Lesser God*. New York: Dramatists Play Service, 1980.

Mojica, Monique. "Theatrical Diversity on Turtle Island." *Canadian Theatre Review* (Fall 1991): 2–3.

Motter, Charlotte. *Theatre in High Schools: Planning, Teaching and Directing*. Englewood Cliffs, N.J.: Prentice Hall, 1970.

Mulcahy, Dennis. "Towards a Theory of Teacher Education in Educational Drama." Ph.D. diss., University of Toronto, 1991.

Ommanney, Katharine, and Harry Schanker. *The Stage and the School*. New York: McGraw-Hill Book Company, 1972.

O'Neill, Cecily. *Drama Guidelines*. London: Heineman Educational Books, 1976.

————. "Artists and Models: Theatre Teachers for the Future." *Design for Arts in Education* 92, no. 4 (March/April 1991): 23–26.

O'Toole, John. *Theatre in Education: New Objectives for Theatre, New Techniques for Education*. London: Hodder & Stoughton, 1976.

Popkewitz, Thomas. "Ideology and Social Formation in Teacher Education." *Teaching and Teacher Education* 1 (1985): 91–107.

————. "Educational Reform: Rhetoric, Ritual, and Social Interest." *Educational Theory* 38, no. 1 (Winter 1988): 77–93.

Quantz, Richard A., and Terence W. O'Connor. "Writing Critical Ethnography: Dialogue, Multivoicedness, and Carnival in Cultural Texts." *Educational Theory* 38, no. 1 (Winter 1988): 95–109.

Reynolds, John, and Malcolm Skilbeck. *Culture and the Classroom*. London: Open Books Publishing Ltd., 1976.

Roose-Evans, James. *Experimental Theatre from Stanislavsky to Peter Brook*. London: Routledge and Kegan Paul, 1984.

Rose, Andrea. "Music Education and the Formation of Social Consciousness." *The Morning Watch* 19, nos. 1–2 (Fall 1991): 47–53.

Ross, Malcolm, ed. *The Development of Aesthetic Experience*. Oxford: Pergamon Press, Ltd., 1982.

Russell, Willy. *Shirley Valentine and One for the Road*. London: Methuen, 1988.

Ryga, George. *The Ecstasy of Rita Joe and Other Plays*. Toronto: New Press, 1971.

Schon, Donald. *The Reflective Practitioner*. New York: Basic Books, 1983.

————. *Educating the Reflective Practitioner*. San Francisco: Jossey-Bass, 1987.

Shaffer, Peter. *Equus*. London: Deutsch, 1973.

Shakespeare, William. *The Complete Plays of William Shakespeare.* New York: Chatham River Press, 1984.

Shaw, Ann W., and C. J. Stevens, eds. *Drama, Theatre and the Handicapped.* New York: American Theatre Association, 1971.

Shuman, R. Baird, ed. *Educational Drama for Today's Schools.* Metuchen, NJ: Scarecrow Press, 1978.

Simon, Roger. "Empowerment as a Pedagogy of Possibility." *Language Arts* 64, no. 4 (1987): 370–82.

Singh, Amarjit. "Reports and Documents on the Quality of Schooling (Part I)." In Amarjit Singh and Ishmael J. Baksh. *Dimensions of Newfoundland Society and Education*, vol. I, 7–23, St. John's: Memorial University of Newfoundland, 1991.

Sizer, T. R. "No Pain, No Gain." *Educational Leadership* 48, no. 8, (1991): 2–34.

Spolin, Viola. *Theater Games for Rehearsal.* Evanston: Northwestern University Press, 1985.

Stoppard, Tom. *Rosencrantz and Guildenstern Are Dead.* New York: Grove Press, 1967.

Verriour, Patrick. "This Is Drama: The Play Beyond the Play." *Language Arts* 66, no. 3 (March 1989): 276–86.

Wagner, B-J. *Dorothy Heathcote: Drama as a Learning Medium.* London: Hutchinson, 1979.

Wasserman, Dale. *One Flew Over the Cuckoo's Nest.* New York: Samuel French, 1974.

Way, Brian. *Development through Drama.* Atlantic Highlands: Humanities Press, 1967.

Webber, Andrew and Tim Rice. *Jesus Christ Superstar.* London: M.C.A. Records, Inc., 1973.

Weiler, Kathleen. *Women Teaching for Change.* New York: Bergin & Garvey, 1988.

Wilder, Rosilyn. *A Space Where Anything Can Happen.* Rowayton: New Play Books, 1977.

Williams, Raymond. *Marxism and Literature.* New York: Oxford University Press, 1977.

————. *The Sociology of Culture.* New York: Schocken Books, 1982.

Willis, Paul. "Cultural Production Is Different from Cultural Reproduction Is Different from Social Reproduction Is Different from Reproduction." *Interchange* 12, no. 49 (1981): 48–67.

Wittrock, M., ed. *Handbook of Research on Teaching.* New York: Macmillian, 1986.

Wolff, Janet. *The Social Production of Art.* New York: New York University Press, 1984.

Wren, Brian. *Education for Justice.* Marynoll: Orbis Books, 1977.

Wright, Lin. "Theatre Education for Everyone." *Design for Arts in Education* 92, no. 4 (1991): 18–20.

Zipes, J., ed. *Political Plays for Children.* Saint Louis: Telos Press, 1976.

Index

About the Author

CLAR DOYLE is Associate Professor of Education at Memorial University of Newfoundland. He has published several articles on the subject of drama and critical pedagogy.